LITERARY
LONDON

LITERARY LONDON

A Book Lover's Guide to the City

**ELOISE MILLAR
& SAM JORDISON**

Michael O'Mara Books Limited

To Polly

This paperback edition first published in 2023
First published in Great Britain in 2016 by
Michael O'Mara Books Limited
9 Lion Yard
Tremadoc Road
London SW4 7NQ

Copyright © Eloise Millar and Sam Jordison 2016, 2023

A CIP catalogue record for this book is available from the British Library.

Papers used by Michael O'Mara Books Limited are natural, recyclable products made
from wood grown in sustainable forests. The manufacturing processes conform to the
environmental regulations of the country of origin.

ISBN: 978-1-78929-593-1 in paperback print format

ISBN: 978-1-78243-505-1 in ebook format

1 2 3 4 5 6 7 8 9 10

Jacket design and inside illustrations by James Nunn

Designed and typeset by Design 23, London

Printed and bound by CPI Group (UK) Ltd, Croydon, CR0 4YY

www.mombooks.com

MIX
Paper | Supporting
responsible forestry
FSC® C171272

CONTENTS

PREFACE

—m—

London is one of the world's greatest literary cities. Its streets are full of stories. Its buildings are steeped in history. Its pubs and clubs are full of writers – and more often than not, are also haunted by their creations.

William Shakespeare, John Milton, Lord Byron, Charles Dickens, Virginia Woolf, Doris Lessing . . . Sherlock Holmes, George Smiley, Sir John Falstaff, Paddington Bear. The biggest and most beloved names in English literature have all been here. You can still see many of their stomping grounds. And this is the book that will tell you how to find them.

As well as explaining where to find the best literary landmarks in London, we aim to tell the stories behind the stories, the moments of inspiration, the formation of friendships – and also the feuds, spats, quarrels and debauches that have always characterized both London and the writing life. We follow Oscar Wilde from his triumph in the city's high-society salons to his humiliation 'in convict dress and handcuffed' on the platform at Clapham Junction. We roam with Julian MacLaren-Ross through Fitzrovia, and drop in for a pint or three with Dylan Thomas at the Bricklayers Arms. We muse darkly over the Thames with Edmund Spenser, T. S. Eliot, Joseph Conrad . . . We see Byron terrorizing his publisher in Albemarle Street – and look on with even greater horror as the same publisher burns the poet's scandalous journals a few years later, on hearing of his death . . .

There are endless tales to tell. It's hard to exaggerate the importance of London as the source, inspiration and theme of much of our finest literature, harder still to imagine how the world of English letters would look without the capital city. After all, it's easy to argue that all literature in English flows directly from the moment Chaucer took up his quill and began to compose *The Canterbury Tales* in London's Aldgate, towards the end of the fourteenth century.

To include every moment in London literary history since then would be impossible. This is by its nature a partial, personal and subjective guide. It may even be eccentric – although we hope that may add to the appeal.

We don't pretend to be comprehensive, but we do aim to be entertaining. Our goal has been to be interesting rather than encyclopedic. Rather than list every street name and road junction, book and poem and person, we've simply included the stories that seem to us the most enlightening and amusing.

We have included plenty of useful addresses too, and there are notes and maps that will provide many days of pleasurable exploring and the heady pleasure of walking the same streets as so many famous writers and characters. Our hope is that you can enjoy the book from beginning to end as a story of the teeming life and inspirational power of this city – but also that you can dip in and out, and use this book to inspire a few good jaunts of your own.

Literary London moves through time and genre, from Edmund Spenser and William Shakespeare to Neil Gaiman and Will Self, from Romantics and diarists to modernists and science-fiction futurists. If you read from beginning to end, you'll have a good overview of London from its distant past as a lonely swampland . . . to its future as pretty much the same thing, if you believe the predictions of many of London's post-apocalyptic authors. Even so, chapters are only loosely chronological, since it's often more fun to group stories by theme rather than by year. We don't aim to be exhaustive. We just try to show why anyone who is tired of London is also – as one writer so famously put it – tired of life.

Eloise Millar and Sam Jordison

CHAPTER ONE

BEGINNERS AND IMMORTALS

—ɱ—

L ondon began in swamp – an empty plain near a wide winding river, surrounded by low hills and not much else. We don't
know when the first houses arrived there, but we do know it
was a long time ago. In 2010 the remains of a large timber building
dating back to 4500 BC were found in the Thames mud, near the present site of Vauxhall Bridge, so we can assume there have been people in the London area for at least 6,000 years, although things remain murky until AD 100, when the settlement became the capital of
Roman Britannia. Even after that there were many dark years. There's
sparse information about Roman London, and even less about what
happened after the collapse of Roman rule, when it's thought that the
city was abandoned. The next good lead comes in the ninth-century
Anglo-Saxon Chronicle, which says that the city was 'refounded' by
Alfred the Great in AD 886.

Alfred was usefully occupied not just in burning cakes, but also
in building and fortifying the wall, developing a new street plan, and
acting as an early literary patron who summoned religious scholars to
translate some of the great Latin works into Old English. Still, the products of any wider literary scene were either sparse, or have been lost in
the mists of time.

Things come into sharper focus in the medieval period. Yet even
then, most early mentions arise in passing. Quite literally so in the case
of Richard of Devizes, a monk from Winchester who walked through
the city sometime in the late twelfth century. He didn't recommend

that others should follow. 'You will come to London,' he wrote. 'Behold! I warn you, whatever of evil or of perversity there is in any, whatever in all parts of the world, you will find in that city alone.' He next provided a long list of all the fun to be had in the area, with its 'effeminate sodomites' and 'lewd musical girls'. Less amusingly, he also became the first person to use the word 'holocaust' in reference to a massacre of the city's Jewish population.

In the same century, William Langland (c.1332–86) grew up and became a 'loller' and 'idler' in the Cornhill area of London. But nothing is certain about his life, since all the information we have comes from the text of his own *Piers Plowman* – a poem where reality is never certain and real life elides with dreams, allegory and mystical Christian quests. This visionary work is thought to have been written in the years between 1370 and 1390, making it contemporary with another great Middle English poem – and the one that is credited with changing and shaping the English language for ever: *The Canterbury Tales*.

It was in London, in the final years of the fourteenth century, that Geoffrey Chaucer (c.1343–1400) produced his long series of stories recounted by pilgrims on their way to Canterbury. Crucially, instead of writing in French or Latin, the dominant literary languages of the time, he chose to compose his verses in a Middle English vernacular – one based on his own London dialect – and so helped set the template for everything that followed.

He also set another useful pattern for London literature by kicking things off in a pub. *The Canterbury Tales* starts in the Tabard on Borough High Street, a real-life tavern which was only pulled down at the end of the nineteenth century. (These days, the site is occupied by a business called 'Copyprints', which seems appropriate for the spiritual home of a work which became in 1478, thanks to William Caxton (1422–91), the first book in English to be printed on a commercial printing press.)

Even though Chaucer's talkative pilgrims soon leave the Tabard and head towards Kent, London makes repeated appearances throughout the narrative. There are references to 'draughts' of 'London ale';

there's chatter about seeking 'chanterys for souls' (endowments for a priest to sing masses) in 'Saint Paul's'; and local taverns in Cheapside and Southwark are name-checked. Madame Eglantine, Chaucer's prioress, also speaks French with a cockney accent – 'And Frenssh she spak ful faire and fetisly, after the scole of Stratford atte Bowe'. ('Fetisly' means fluently, 'scole' is school . . . You will easily work out the rest.)

And then there's the fact that Chaucer was a Londoner himself. He was probably born in the city around 1343, and his father and grandfather were established London vintners. The latter was murdered near his house in Aldgate in 1313, a time when the area was notorious for its after-dark thefts, rapes and murders. Luckily, Chaucer survived, and lived for much of his life at 2 Aldgate High Street, in a twin-towered gatehouse that he got free of rent on the proviso that he allowed troops to use the towers in time of attack. (Which means that they presumably used it in 1381, when Wat Tyler and his angry followers stormed into the capital from the countryside during the Peasants' Revolt (see p. 27), passing directly under Chaucer's windows.)

Chaucer was a busy man. He worked as a courtier, diplomat, civil servant, and Clerk of the King's Works. He also studied law at the Inner Temple – and who knows how he also made time to write *The Canterbury Tales* (especially after 1374, when Edward III granted him a daily 'gallon of wine' for the rest of his life). Yet he managed it, producing endless ribald jokes and thousands of lines of exquisite poetry. He continued to work on *The Canterbury Tales* almost until the day he died.

Chaucer's last years were spent in Somerset, but he moved back to the capital in 1399, taking a lease on a residence within the close of Westminster Abbey. He also became the first person to be buried in Poets' Corner, a stone's throw from his home, in late 1400. Very few other landmarks from Chaucer's time remain: the closest you'll get are St Paul's (although the building Chaucer knew was destroyed in the Great Fire) and St Botolph Aldgate (which, while it has also been remodelled, has stood on the same spot for over 1,000 years). If you want to get a taste for something a little less devout, head over to

Southwark's Borough High Street, where at number 77 you'll find the George, the only remaining coaching inn in London, and pleasingly close to the site of Chaucer's Tabard.

> **'The city of London, that is to me so dear and sweet, in which I was forth growen; and more kindly love have I to that place than to any other on earth.'**
>
> Geoffrey Chaucer, *The Testament of Love*

Less keen on drink was Margery Kempe (*c.*1373–*c.*1438). She was a religious mystic from King's Lynn who chronicled her many pilgrimages, conversations with God and arguments with unworthy men in her great work of autobiography and visionary fiction, *The Book of Margery Kempe*. She also made a few visits to London. The first time around, she went in poverty, dressed in sackcloth. Happily, she was well received by pious widows and was soon out and about speaking 'boldly and strongly' to the capital's many 'cursers, liars, swearers' and 'vicious people'. These strong speeches apparently profited 'many people very much'. On a later visit she stayed in London 'a long time' and was 'well received by many worthy men' – which was a welcome advance on the humiliation and reproof she often found on her travels through medieval England.

Following Kempe's came another great prose work with a London connection, Thomas Malory's *Le Morte D'Arthur*. At least, we think it was by Malory – the facts are hazy. The Malory in question didn't always live in London, but spent his early years around Warwickshire, cattle-raiding and committing more serious crimes like rape and murder. However, he did spend several years in London's Newgate Prison in the 1460s, and it's there that scholars think he wrote his great work of swords and chivalry, before his death in 1471.

Popular as Malory's Arthurian legends may have been, poetry was still regarded as the highest form of literature, and when Edmund Spenser (*c.* 1552–99) wrote *The Faerie Queene*, his epic hymn of praise to Queen Elizabeth I, he did so in verse form.

Perhaps unsurprising for a man best known for asking the 'sweet Thames' to 'run softly', Spenser spent most of his adult life outside London. It's most likely, in fact, that he wrote *The Faerie Queene* in Ireland, sometime between 1590 and 1596. But he had been born in London, in East Smithfield, as well as educated at the Merchant Taylors' School (which then lay within the city walls), and he travelled to London to publish and promote his book.

He died in London too – and did so in poverty (for 'want of bread' is how Ben Jonson put it) – even though Elizabeth I, as reward for *The Faerie Queene*, had granted Spenser £50 a year for the rest of his life – a considerable sum in the sixteenth century. Whether this was never actually paid or he managed to fritter it away is open to speculation; either way, when he was forty-seven he joined Chaucer in Poets' Corner.

Another pupil of the Merchant Taylors' School (and contemporary to Spenser) was Thomas Kyd (1558–94), who wrote the first revenge tragedy: *The Spanish Tragedy*, first performed in 1592. In 1593 he shared a lodging room with his fellow playwright Christopher Marlowe (1564–93), probably in Norton Folgate or Shoreditch, where all of the fashionable actors lived. It was there that Kyd was arrested and brutally tortured after a search of his and Marlowe's room uncovered literature unpalatable to the local authorities.

At the time, libellous pamphlets had been making the rounds in London. These were signed 'Tamburlaine', the name of Marlowe's most famous character, and because of their content and signature, surveillance had homed in on the theatrical world. A warrant was issued for Marlowe's arrest, too; he was killed (supposedly in a brawl) twelve days later. Kyd was released, but as a broken man, who died the following year. His mother buried him at St Mary Colechurch in the City of London (located at 82 Cheapside and burned down in the Great Fire of London; an Alliance & Leicester office now stands on the site).

As for Christopher Marlowe (to borrow a metaphor from one of his famous contemporaries), his candle burned brief, but it shone bright. During the six years he was writing plays (from 1587 until

1593) he produced immortal classics like *Tamburlaine the Great* and *Doctor Faustus* – crucial works in a new and daring age of literature. Marlowe was one of the first to use blank verse, and for his literary talent alone was revered by those around him (including Shakespeare, who borrowed at least 100 lines of Marlowe's and used them in his own plays).

Marlowe was relentlessly controversial, repeatedly crossing the lines in what could and couldn't be said, whether on the monarchy or religion (he may have been an atheist). He also, arguably, wrote Britain's first homosexual love story in *Edward II*, which dealt with the star-crossed romance of Edward and Piers Gaveston. Many think it was this kind of troublemaking that earned him a knife thrust in the eye.

After his death, Marlowe was buried in an unmarked grave in St Nicholas Church, Deptford, where a memorial plaque is dedicated to him on the churchyard wall. But even if he was buried anonymously, his legacy has lived on. His life has also inspired new works of literature, in books like *Dead Man in Deptford* by Anthony Burgess (1917–93) – evidence of how much myth-making has gathered around Marlowe.

Burgess's novel is also a fine survey of the city in Marlowe's time, should you be interested – and you should be, because London in the 1580s and 1590s was something special. In 1400 the population had been around 50,000. By the late sixteenth century it had swelled to over 200,000 and was still soaring. A Swiss visitor to London at the time declared: 'One simply cannot walk for the crowds.' The playwright and pamphleteer Thomas Dekker (1572–1632) gave a vivid description of the noise and bustle in his pamphlet *The Seven Deadly Sins of London*:

> Carts and coaches make such a thundering din as if the world ran on wheels; at every corner men, women, and children meet in such shoals that posts are set up to strengthen the houses lest with jostling with one another they should shoulder them down. Besides, hammers are beating in one place, tubs hooping in another [the noise made by coopers or barrel

makers], pots clinking in a third, water-tankards running at tilt
in a fourth ... Tradesmen, as if they were dancing galliards are
lusty at legs and never stand still ...

Dekker, who is sometimes seen as a precursor to Dickens in his
depictions of the smoky, pest-ridden and yet gloriously energetic
capital, was a prolific author. Not even imprisonment in Southwark
(at the King's Bench) for debt – and for seven whole years – appeared
to stop him, and he's one of the best sources we have for London life
during Shakespeare's era. Plays like *The Shoemaker's Holiday* take in the
lives of normal Londoners; his pamphlet *The Wonderful Yeare* provides
a vivid journalistic account of London during a plague outbreak (as
well as of the death of Elizabeth I and ascension of James I). *Newes
from Hell* and *The Seven Deadly Sins of London* deliver a judgement on
the city, but also an affectionate portrait of the ebullient daily life of
the streets.

Though it wasn't just the streets that mattered in early modern
London. The Thames – running through the surging, thronging
powerhouse of the capital – was never quite as sweet as Spenser
claimed. In fact, refuse and sewage impeded its flow. But the river
must still have been something to behold. It was wider than today,
lined with stairs and landings on both banks, and thronged with barg-
es and ferries (one of which probably took Shakespeare to the theatre
in Southwark on most days) ... Sometimes it froze over and frost fairs
were held on the ice (as recalled by Virginia Woolf (1882–1941) in
Orlando), complete with dancing, stalls selling food and drink, and on
one notable occasion in 1564 attended by Queen Elizabeth I herself.
There was only one bridge – London Bridge – from which there
occasionally protruded, on iron spikes, the rotting heads of traitors.

London Bridge led to Southwark and Bankside, an area which had
a reputation for trouble. As well as the stamping ground of writers and
intellectuals, it was the haunt of bear-baiters, cutpurses, prostitutes and
highwaymen, not to mention the location of a good half-dozen jails
(such as the infamously cruel Clink) and countless taverns. But it was

also a booming commercial zone, full of markets, travellers and merchants. Rich men lived there too – and had done for years. One John Falstaff, for instance, built a mansion there in the 1450s, and so left Shakespeare a fine name to borrow more than a century later.

Southwark was also the home of the theatres, thanks to the fun-hating Puritans who wouldn't let playhouses be built inside the city walls. To get around this, the earliest plays in the city were performed in the courtyards of inns (and the galleried yard of the George Inn in Southwark, again, gives a good impression of how the space would have worked). It was only a matter of time, however, before the need for a proper theatre was addressed. In 1574 the impresario James Burbage (1530–97) received a licence to perform plays, but so much heat was turned up against him by vociferous clergy that he had to flee the city. (One letter ran: 'The cause of plagues is sin, if you look to it well, and the cause of sin are plays: therefore the cause of plagues are plays.') Burbage retreated to the Liberty of Shoreditch (at that point just outside London; these days, Zone 1), where he managed, in 1576, with the help of his brother and outside the jurisdiction of the preachers, to erect what was to become the first permanent playhouse in England, called, reasonably enough, 'The Theatre'. It's commemorated by a brown plaque on 86–88 Curtain Road.

The Theatre held around 1,000 people, and was so successful that another venue called the Curtain was opened next to it a year later. After this, the centre of gravity moved south of the Thames when

John Taylor (1578–1653) was a Thames waterman who liked to call himself 'The Water Poet' – and who, among other things, wrote verses about cannabis. In his *The Praise of Hemp-Seed*, Taylor's passion for the herb rivals that of any modern-day activist: 'The profits arising by Hemp-seed are/Cloathing, Food, Fishing, Shipping/Pleasure, Profit, Justice, Whipping.' It was possibly enjoyment of hemp's other benefits that led to some of Taylor's more eccentric activities, such as attempting to row from London to Queensborough in a paper boat.

Philip Henslowe built the Rose in Southwark in 1587. Burbage's theatre eventually followed – in a very literal way. When its Shoreditch lease ran out in 1598, Burbage's sons had its timbers carried across the river to Park Street on Bankside, close to the Rose. The Theatre was renamed the Globe (affectionately dubbed this 'wooden O' by Shakespeare), and the next few years saw the first performances of immortal classics like *Hamlet*, *Othello* and *Macbeth*.

In June 1613, during a performance of Shakespeare's last play, *Henry VIII*, a cannon was fired and a stray spark landed on the theatre's thatched roof. The Globe burned to the ground – though, amazingly, none of the 3,000-strong audience were injured (except one man whose trousers caught fire; he was successfully doused with tankards of beer). It was rebuilt – with a tiled roof – and remained in business right up until 1642, when the Puritans finally got their way and closed all theatres in the city.

The Globe was turned into tenement flats and eventually disappeared. Its remaining foundations are buried, though you can see them marked out on today's Park Street by coloured stones. Round the corner, near Rose Alley (which in Shakespeare's day was an open sewer), you can also see the remains of the Rose Theatre. These foundations were discovered in 1989 when the site was being cleared for offices; when excavations began, the exposure to air caused the old oak beams to rot, so these days the site is kept submerged in water (oak swells in water, and is better preserved). The outline of the Rose's walls is picked out in red lights, making it an atmospheric, eerie place to visit (and to listen to the readings often held there).

One piece of Shakespearean authenticity from which we

are thankfully spared is the smell. Those who bought the cheapest tickets for the theatre didn't have any toilet facilities . . . so they resorted to the ground. A popular slang term used to refer to them was 'stinkards'. In spite of such snobbery – according to the renowned critic Harold Bloom – this was probably the first and last time in British history that theatre was truly democratic. It was affordable for everyone, with tiered pricing, from the standing-room places (in the 'pitt', bought by 'groundlings') to the seated galleries, and attended by all, from high to low. It's never been the same ever since – or arguably as vibrant. Stephen Gosson (1554–1624) painted a vivid picture of play-going culture at the time in *Playes Confuted in Five Actions*:

> In the playhouses at London, it is the fashion of youths to go first into the yard, and to carry their eye through every gallery, then like ravens, where they spy the carrion thither they fly, and press as near to the fairest as they can . . . they give them apples, they dally with their garments to pass the time, they minister talk upon odd occasions, and either bring them home to their houses on small acquaintance, or slip into taverns when the plays are done.

Southwark continued to grow as an entertainment centre throughout Gosson's lifetime and beyond. At its height in Jacobean London there were around twenty theatres to choose from. But they weren't the only source of entertainment. Several important inns and pubs in the city walls functioned as playhouses (as well as lodgings for the actors): The Bull (off Bishopsgate), the Cross Keys Inn (on Gracechurch Street), the Bel Savage (off Ludgate Hill) and the Bell Inn Yarde (off Gracechurch Street).

You probably won't be surprised to learn that playwrights also liked to drink in pubs. The Anchor on Bankside (34 Park Street) can lay a good claim to being one of Shakespeare's locals. It survived the Great Fire of London (Pepys watched some of the progress of the conflagration from there), but was rebuilt in 1676, so you won't get an entirely authentic experience by visiting, even if it remains wooden-beamed and evocative.

Sadly, there's nothing to be seen of another favoured drinking haunt of playwrights and actors, the Mermaid Tavern. This is one of the tens (maybe hundreds) of pubs that actually did burn down in the fire. East of St Paul's Cathedral and on the corner of Friday Street and Bread Street, the Mermaid was the headquarters of a drinking club called the 'Fraternity of Sireniacal Gentlemen', which met on the first Friday of every month and boasted members including John Donne (1572–1631), Ben Jonson (1572–1637) and John Fletcher (1579–1625) . . . (Some scholars like to include Shakespeare, but this is stretching it a bit.) The nearby (tiny) Mitre is mentioned in Jonson's *Bartholomew Fair*, and has a preserved tree in the bar which Elizabeth I reportedly danced around one May Day.

Bartholomew Fair is Jonson's great London play, and uses as its setting the annual summer fair in Smithfield (with its combination of market stalls and entertainments) to offer something of a panorama of modern London life, with pickpockets, bullies, upstanding lawmen, Puritans and pimps. First performed in 1614, it remained popular for most of the rest of the century. Samuel Pepys loved it so much that he went to see it four times in 1661.

The actual Bartholomew Fair came under the hammer of the City authorities in 1855, when they outlawed it for encouraging debauchery and public disorder. It was, according to the *Newgate Calendar*, 'a school of vice which has initiated more youth into the habits of villainy than Newgate itself'.

Jonson was another leading light of his age – and someone we know quite a bit about. He first went to school in St Martin's Lane, Covent Garden – near, appropriately enough, what is today London's Theatreland – and then went on to Westminster School. After that he was an apprentice to his stepfather, who was a master bricklayer. As part of his training, he built a garden wall in Lincoln's Inn, but clearly building walls was too confining, because he next took off to the Continent for a spell as a soldier, before returning to London and taking up work as both an actor and a playwright. One of his first performances was in Thomas Kyd's *The Spanish Tragedy*.

The most notable Jonson landmark in the city is the Church of St Magnus the Martyr (in the City of London), where he married Ann Lewis in 1594. There he also recorded the deaths of two of his children: Mary Jonson at six months, in 1593, and Benjamin Jonson, in 1603, at seven years old, of bubonic plague. 'Farewell, thou child of my right hand, and joy,' Jonson wrote, in lines that will break any parent's heart: 'Rest in soft peace, and ask'd, say, here doth lye/Ben Jonson his best piece of poetry.'

By summer 1597 Jonson was permanently employed by the Admiral's Men, a group of actors who were performing under Philip Henslowe at the Rose on Bankside. In the same year, Jonson also co-wrote a play with Thomas Nashe (1567–1601). It was called *The Isle of Dogs* and no copies survive, so we can only guess at what it was about, but it vexed the Virgin Queen so profoundly that Jonson was thrown into Southwark's Marshalsea Prison, charged with 'lewde and mutinous behaviour' (Nashe managed to escape to Great Yarmouth).

This trouble didn't halt Jonson's inclination towards making fun of his peers and writing plays about high-level corruption. He was popped back into prison for another seditious play – also lost – shortly after the play's first performance in October 1605. A few weeks later he was also present at a London dinner attended by most of the members of the Gunpowder Plot.

This must have brought him up short, however, because from then on he became a little more circumspect. He took to writing masques (combinations of script, spectacle and dance) for the Court, and on 1 January 1611, in collaboration with the famous architect and set designer Inigo Jones, he presented *Oberon, the Faerie Prince* to Whitehall, with James I's son appearing in the title role. Happily, Jonson managed to keep his sense of humour in spite of such blatant fawning. One of his

It wasn't just Ben Jonson who liked to snipe at fellow playwrights. Many of his targets sniped right back, and in 1590s London what has since become known as the 'War of the Theatres' (later dubbed 'Poetomachia' by Thomas Dekker) broke out, when the point-scoring got out of control. In *Jack Drum's Entertainment*, John Marston satirized Jonson as a cuckold. Then, after Jonson portrayed both Marston and Dekker as 'arrogating puffs' and 'voluptuous revellers' in *Cynthia's Revels*, Jonson found himself appearing in both *What You Will* and *Satiromastix* as an arrogant, overbearing hypocrite . . . The squabbles seem to have died down by 1604, when Marston dedicated *The Malcontent* to Jonson, with whom he was buddies again.

later plays, *The Alchemist*, for instance, featured a trio of London hucksters glorying in the names of Subtle, Doll Common and Captain Face.

Talking of glory, of course there's no outshining William Shakespeare, the brightest star of early modern London or any other age. Stratford may be able to claim him as its native son, but he spent most of his adult life – a wonderfully prolific twenty-odd years – in London.

Between 1589 and 1613 Shakespeare wrote around thirty-eight plays (the exact number is disputed), 154 sonnets and at least two long narrative poems. In the process he changed what it means to be (or not to be) human. It's impossible to think of a world without his poetry – or to conceive what a Shakespeare-shaped gap would mean to English civilization and beyond.

It's also impossible to think of London without Shakespeare, even if much of his life in the city is a matter of conjecture. We don't know anything definite about Shakespeare's lodgings, for instance. But we do have a general idea, and can place his comings and goings around the city, east London, and Bankside. During the late 1590s he lodged somewhere in Bishopsgate, in the parish of St Helen's in the vicinity of Leadenhall and St Mary Avenue. Later, in 1604, he lived in Silver Street, St Paul's, in the upstairs room of the house of the Mountjoys, a well-to-do Huguenot family. We know that he lived there for quite a while, because he became entangled in a court case between his landlord and the landlord's son-in-law.

That house was destroyed in the Great Fire, and most of its surroundings levelled in the Blitz. (The whole area was redeveloped after the Second World War, and these days Silver Street is no more. But if you go to the corner of London Wall and Noble Street to the north of St Paul's, you'll have a good chance of walking in Shakespeare's footsteps.) In 1613, by then a wealthy man, he was in a position to buy a house outright. This he did, and for £140: it was known as The Gatehouse and located in Ireland Yard, the north-eastern corner of the old Blackfriars Priory. He never lived there and on his death left the house to his daughter Susanna. (These days, the site boasts the small and cosy Cockpit Pub.)

We also know that by 1591 Shakespeare had written his first play, *The Comedy of Errors*, and that soon after he turned to writing sonnets, partly because an outbreak of plague closed the London theatres for two years, from 1592 to 1594. Having less to do than usual, he started comparing his amorous other to a summer's day and writing immortal love poetry.

When the theatres reopened, Shakespeare joined Burbage's company, the Lord Chamberlain's Men, which – for obvious reasons – soon became the most popular in the city. Burbage's son Richard was the leading actor, and he was the first to play many of Shakespeare's famous characters. It wasn't all sweetness and light for Shakespeare, however. In 1596, his eleven-year-old son Hamnet died. Many think that the grief of this death helped inspire Shakespeare's most famous tragedy, *Hamlet*, written sometime between 1599 and 1602.

It's possible to trace other inspirations too. In 1600 a delegation arrived in London from Morocco, four years before the first performance of *Othello, the Moor of Venice*. There's also an enjoyable theory that the 'Dark Lady' of Shakespeare's sonnets (whom he also calls 'my female evil' and 'my bad angel') was actually based on a bawdy-house madam who lived in Clerkenwell called 'Lucy Negro' or 'Black Luce'. What we do know for sure is that Philip Henslowe (the owner of the Rose Theatre) was friends with Lucy's close business associate Gilbert East, and that they dined together frequently (East was also employed as Henslowe's bailiff). So the circles were definitely connected. She's also mentioned by several of Shakespeare's other acquaintances – and when *The Comedy of Errors* was staged at the Clerkenwell Inns of Court (notorious for their somewhat licentious Christmas entertainments) in 1594, Black Luce was recorded as a member of the audience.

In contrast – and more certainly – it's also known that Shakespeare worshipped at Southwark Cathedral, where a reclining statue of the bard was installed in 1912, along with a stained-glass window depicting scenes from his plays. Shakespeare's younger brother Edmund was buried there in 1607, and Philip Henslowe in 1616.

Shakespeare himself was buried in Stratford in the same year as Henslowe, having retired there sometime around 1613, a rich and successful man. In his later years, one of his most regular gigs had been performing a good dozen times a year in front of King James I – at Whitehall Palace, for instance. Sadly, you can't go to this site, as most of the building was destroyed by fire in 1698. If you want to go somewhere Shakespeare and his players actually trod the boards, book an appointment to see the interior of Middle Temple Hall. This is London's greatest Tudor interior – it dates from 1572 – and *King Lear* was performed there several times. On 2 February 1602, the first recorded performance of *Twelfth Night* also took place there.

Equally worth visiting is the reconstructed Globe. If you're there around 23 April (the presumed date of Shakespeare's birthday), the theatre puts on two guided walks, called 'Sweet Love Remember'd', that take in the South Bank and Shakespeare's old haunts. Visit the Guildhall too, which was around in Shakespeare's day and houses one of the precious First Folios of his plays.

Curiously, if you're looking for direct connections to Shakespeare's London, you won't get much help from his plays. They tell us a lot about his times and customs indirectly, but there aren't that

The Globe Theatre ('Shakespeare's Globe'), currently sitting on the South Bank of the Thames, was opened for performances in 1997. It is a faithful reconstruction of the original theatre initiated by the actor and director Sam Wanamaker (1919-93) and based on academic ideas about the original building.

many straight references to the city. Although contemporaries like Ben Jonson wrote popular, up-to-date city comedies, Shakespeare avoided setting any of his in London during his own time. When he mentioned the place directly, it was mainly in history plays – in the two parts of *Henry IV*, for instance, Falstaff enjoys quaffing sack and carousing at the Boar's Head in Eastcheap. Richard III arranges the murder of his brother Clarence and his nephews in the Tower of London. In *Henry VIII* the trial of Katherine of Aragon takes place in Blackfriars. Shakespeare got reasonably close to London in one comedy, *The Merry Wives of Windsor*, but that too was ostensibly set during the reign of Henry IV (which is why Falstaff is able to play a welcome cameo). Otherwise, the nearest he got to the capital outside the history plays was Lear's blasted heath and the few moments when the action in *Macbeth* strays south of the Scottish border.

Yet while Shakespeare didn't write all that much about London, there's no doubt that he thrived and flourished there. It was his home, his living and his inspiration – and as such it deserves our eternal gratitude.

KEY ADDRESSES

Poets' Corner, Westminster Abbey, Dean's Yard, SW1P (Tube station: Westminster)

The George Inn, The George Inn Yard, 77 Borough High Street, SE1 (Tube station: London Bridge)

The Anchor, 34 Park Street, SE1 (Tube station: London Bridge)

The Clink Prison, 1 Clink Street, SE1 (Tube station: London Bridge)

Shakespeare's Bankside

Bankside

1 Southwark Cathedral
2 The Anchor
3 The Globe Theatre
4 The Hope Theatre
5 Bear Baiting
6 The Rose Theatre
7 The Bull Ring
8 The Swan Theatre

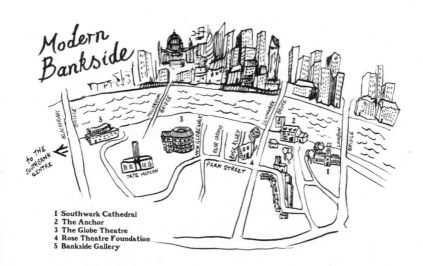

Modern Bankside

1 Southwark Cathedral
2 The Anchor
3 The Globe Theatre
4 Rose Theatre Foundation
5 Bankside Gallery

The Rose Theatre Trust, 56 Park Street, SE1 (Tube station: London Bridge)

Shakespeare's Globe, 21 New Globe Walk, SE1 (Tube station: London Bridge)

The Tower of London, Tower Hill, EC3N (Tube station: Tower Hill)

Ye Olde Mitre Tavern, 1 Ely Place, EC1N (Tube station: Farringdon)

Banqueting House, Whitehall, SW1A (Tube station: Westminster)

Middle Temple Hall, Middle Temple Lane, EC4Y (Tube station: Temple)

Guildhall, Gresham Street, EC2P (Tube station: Moorgate)

RECOMMENDED READING

Anthony Burgess, *Nothing Like the Sun*; *Dead Man in Deptford*

Geoffrey Chaucer, *The Canterbury Tales*

Ben Jonson, *Bartholomew Fair*

Christopher Marlowe, *Tamburlaine the Great*

William Shakespeare, *Complete Works*

James Shapiro, *1599: A Year in the Life of William Shakespeare*

CHAPTER TWO
RADICALS AND SUBVERSIVES

—⚎—

n 1381, in Blackheath, the hedge priest John Ball (1338–81) ('hedge priest' because he did his preaching on the roads, outside conventional churches) uttered the famous couplet:

When Adam delved and Eve span,
Who was then the gentleman?

And so he provided one of the earliest contributions to the long tradition of radical agitation in London. Ball went on to declare that 'all men by nature were created alike, and our bondage or servitude came in by the unjust oppression of naughty men', and to exhort his listeners to revolution. Naturally, the royal authorities weren't keen on these ideas – and summarily chopped off his head, displaying it on a spike on London Bridge.

They soon had plenty of other heads to display. After the meeting at Blackheath, a great crowd of disgruntled peasants, led by a roof-tiler called Wat Tyler, stomped over London Bridge and up to Aldgate (presumably passing Chaucer's house on the way). The rebels fomented further revolt by sending letters around the country, many of them signed in the name of Piers Plowman, inspired by passages in Langland's poem about the 'saintly' hard-working peasant. They also managed to wreck the Savoy Palace and kill the Lord Chancellor in the Tower of London before they were brutally suppressed. More than 1,500 rebels were killed.

The one surviving eyewitness account of the Peasants' Revolt, written by an anonymous member of the court in London, is called the *Anonimalle Chronicle*. It stresses – among other things – that the rebels against taxation and serfdom were nasty, dirty countrymen, and certainly not from London.

In spite of such bad press, the revolt continued to inspire popular uprisings. Most notably, some 300 years later Ball would influence the Levellers – the seventeenth-century, London-born revolutionary group thrown up by the chaos of the English Civil War. Demanding equality before the law, popular sovereignty, extended suffrage and religious tolerance, the Levellers were also pretty good with their pens, publishing a wealth of pamphlets that gloried in titles like *England's Lamentable Slaverie* and *A Remonstrance of Many Thousand Citizens*. They met in pubs in Islington; one called the Rosemary Branch, its name taken from the sprigs of the herb that Levellers wore in their hats to identify themselves (there's still a Rosemary Branch pub in Islington today – but not in the same place). Most famously, they held a series of debates at the Church of St Mary the Virgin, Putney, in October and November 1647, resulting in that classic of political agitation, *The Agreement of the People*. They also handed a petition in to parliament that was signed by a third of all Londoners. In spite – or quite possibly because – of such popularity, by 1649 most of the leaders had been killed or imprisoned, and their pamphlets were all that remained of them.

During the same period, while living in Aldersgate Street just outside the City of London, John Milton also wrote his broadside *Areopagitica*, pleading for freedom from censorship. With predictable irony, it fell foul of the censors and had to be distributed secretly.

Milton at least survived long enough to write *Paradise Lost*, even after going completely blind. Many of London's other revolutionaries did not fare so well. One of the most tragic was Mary Wollstonecraft (1759–97). In 1792 she wrote *A Vindication of the Rights of Woman* (a partial and wonderfully cheeky reply to her friend Thomas Paine's *The Rights of Man*, written a year earlier in the Angel Inn, Islington). Here, brilliantly, she made a point that seems obvious now, but staggered many of her contemporaries: that women were quite as clever as men, and the only thing holding them back was a lack of proper education. But Wollstonecraft also suffered from depression – and from unreliable partners. In 1795, abandoned by Gilbert Imlay (1754–1828), an American diplomat and the father of her young child, she threw herself off Putney Bridge. 'When you receive this,' she wrote in her suicide note, 'my burning head will be cold . . . I shall plunge into the Thames, where there is least chance of my being snatched from the death I seek.'

Even here she was unfortunate. She was rescued by a passer-by.

By 1796, Wollstonecraft had at least found a share of happiness with William Godwin (1756–1836). They set up shop together, living (at first, scandalously, 'in sin') in apartments at 29 The Polygon, a pleasant crescent of houses near King's Cross, just behind the current site of the British Library. (The street has long since been knocked down, but at the time it initiated the area's links with France when it housed many people fleeing the French Revolution.) Sadly, after just one year, the birth of her daughter Mary (Shelley – she of *Frankenstein* fame) would leave Wollstonecraft with blood poisoning. She never recovered, and died within ten days.

Sixty years later, Karl Marx (1818–83) sat in the old British Library building on Great Russell Street, in seat L13, writing *Das Kapital*. (Fifty years later again, Vladimir Lenin (1870–1924) visited the same seat. He signed in as 'Jacob Richter', and was seen by the poet John Masefield (1878–1967), who wondered 'who that extraordinary man was'.)

When he wasn't slaving over his manuscript, Marx liked to help himself to food and wine at his friend Friedrich Engels's (1820–95) house on Soho's Dean Street. This location was doubly fortunate, as it made it easy, on Marx's way home from a day's writing, for him to grab a final drink at the nearby Black Horse, where he was known for climbing on tables and making speeches.

In fact, Marx had rather a penchant for bar-room philosophy. And heavy drinking. Wilhelm Liebknecht (1826–1900), a German republican revolutionary, was a friend of Marx when he lived in London in the 1850s, and wrote a book called *Biographical Memoirs* about him in 1901. In it he recalls a night in the late 1850s when he and Marx and a fellow German political philosopher, Edgar Bauer (1820–86), went out on the razzle in central London.

'The problem,' wrote Liebknecht, 'was to "take something" in every saloon between Oxford Street and Hampstead Road.' No easy task, since that part of the city was full of pubs. 'But we went to work undaunted,' he continued, 'and managed to reach the end of Tottenham Court Road without accident.'

Here they entered another pub and joined a raucous crowd. They all talked merrily – until Marx gave a lecture about the fact that England had no art to compare to Beethoven. 'The brows of our hosts began to cloud,' said Liebknecht, so the philosophers beat a retreat. They'd had enough of pubs and started walking home to Highgate. On the way, the renowned Hegelian Bauer spotted a heap of paving stones, shouted 'Hurrah, an idea!' and started putting out gaslights. Marx and Liebknecht joined in, attracting the attention of several policemen, who gave chase. The three Germans dashed off down a back alley. 'Marx showed an activity that I should not have attributed to him,' said Liebknecht, and the three made it home 'without further adventures'.

Another Marx local, the Red Lion of Soho, can be found at 20 Great Windmill Street, where he lectured in 1847 and, with Engels, wrote an 'action programme' for the Communist League. But if you aren't

Karl Marx is buried in Highgate Cemetery in north London. On his tombstone are the words: 'The philosophers have only interpreted the world in various ways. The point however is to change it.'

feeling thirsty, Marx is also well commemorated in Clerkenwell's Marx Memorial Library and Workers' School – a lovely eighteenth-century building that used to be the location of the Twentieth Century Press, a socialist publisher founded by the Social Democratic Federation. Lenin worked there for a year during his exile.

> **'Ilyich [Lenin] studied living London. He liked taking long rides through the town on top of the bus. He liked the busy traffic of that vast commercial city. There were other places too – mean little streets tenanted by London's work people, with clothes lines stretched across the roads and anemic children playing on the doorsteps . . . Ilyich would mutter in English through clenched teeth: "Two nations!"'**
>
> Lenin's wife, Krupskaya Lenin, reminiscing on their time in the capital

Marx and Engels weren't the only radicals on the streets of nineteenth-century London. In 1826 the author William Cobbett (1763–1835) made his famous speech against the Corn Laws on Clerkenwell Green. In 1887 George Bernard Shaw (1856–1950) and the pre-Raphaelite painter and writer William Morris (1834–96) set off for Trafalgar Square in a huge protest against coercion and unemployment in Ireland. There, on 13 November, they witnessed Bloody Sunday – when police and protesters clashed, 75 people were injured and 400 arrested.

Also in Trafalgar Square, George Orwell (1903–50) slept rough in the 1920s. He later renamed it Victory Square, a major site of oppression in his novel *Nineteen Eighty-Four*, by way of thanks. London locations peppered his story of revolution gone horribly wrong. He based

Friedrich Engels's first apartment in London, at 28 Dean Street, was also the sometime lodgings of Karl Marx – and is these days home to the upmarket restaurant Quo Vadis, with a private room dedicated to Marx which can be rented out for 'corporate drinks'.

parts of the Ministry of Truth canteen on the windowless canteen at the BBC (at 200 Oxford Street) and the rest on the Senate House in the University of London. Orwell's own revolutionary activities were mainly carried out on paper while he was in London – although he was frequently thrown out of the Acropolis Restaurant at 24 Percy Street in the 1940s. His crime? Not wearing a jacket. (Once, when dining there with Malcolm Muggeridge, he asked to swap seats, so that he didn't have to look at the 'corrupt face' of *New Statesman* editor Kingsley Martin, who had taken the side of the Stalinists in the Spanish Civil War.)

'I came to London and in a few months I was a Trotskyist.'

C. L. R. James

Clerkenwell Green's left-leaning credentials run far back. Before its early 1900s incarnation as the home of a socialist publisher, the Marx Memorial Library was a charitable school for Welsh paupers; in the 1790s the offices of numerous anti-war and political movements were housed around the Green, and in his novel *Demos: A Story of English Socialism*, George Gissing gives the area a prominent role. In the early 1800s there was also a barber's-cum-coffee-house-cum-reading room called Lunt's, a regular meeting point of the Chartists and a place where you could grab a cup of coffee, get your hair cut and listen to a lecture against slavery (delivered with some passion by the owner) all at once.

So far, so leftist – but literary London has played host to all shades of opinion. Diana Mitford (1910–2003) was probably its most notorious fascist writer-in-residence during the blackshirt era of the 1930s and 40s, but there have also been others with unpalatable beliefs. One of the most curious groupings centred on Colin Wilson (1931–2013), author of the unexpected philosophical hit *The Outsider* (1956), and his fellow writers Bill Hopkins (1928–2011) and John Braine (1922–86), at 25 Chepstow Road in Notting Hill. Wilson believed in a unique brand of English existentialism; he maintained that only 5 per cent of humanity were equipped to use political power, and that these supermen should be allowed to rule everyone else. According to the writer Peter Vansittart, shortly after *The Outsider* was released, a woman questioned him on these beliefs, and his intellectual snobbery, at an event in the Institute for Contemporary Arts.

'Mr Wilson – I do not consider myself an intellectual,' she said. 'I have a beautiful home and a well-kept garden, a loving husband and two friendly well-behaved boys. Please tell me in all seriousness where I have gone wrong.'

Wilson replied: 'You . . . You're the worst of the lot! Unspeakable! A mainstream criminal! Of course you enjoy simple things, you're incapable of anything else. Your house is garbage, your garden a midden and a swamp, your husband is Gordon Fitzhomo and your children are dung . . . You're the dregs of the country, barely conceivable in your enormity, and it's appalling that you were ever conceived.'

No one said that debate has always been decorous.

KEY ADDRESSES

Church of St Mary the Virgin, High Street, SW15 (Tube station: Putney Bridge)
The Angel, 3–5 Islington High Street, N1 (Tube station: Angel)
Trafalgar Square, WC2N (Tube station: Charing Cross)
Senate House, University of London, Malet Street, WC1E (Tube station: Russell Square)

RECOMMENDED READING

Karl Marx, *Das Kapital*
George Orwell, *Nineteen Eighty-Four*
Thomas Paine, *The Rights of Man*
Mary Wollstonecraft, *A Vindication of the Rights of Woman*

CHAPTER THREE
PREACHERS AND CONVERTS

—◁ɯ▷—

Many writers may be rebels, but piety also runs through London's literary history. Long after the visit of Margery Kempe and after the Prioress and the Monk told their stories in *The Canterbury Tales* by Chaucer, religious men and women have featured big in fact and fiction. They have overseen countless weddings and funerals in novels and poems, stalked – black-cloaked and severe in aspect – through dozens of Victorian novels, and bored generations of fictional schoolchildren.

Yet the religious have not always been a boon to literary writers. Many of the Church's most notable contributions to London literary history have come in the form of attempts to suppress plays, novels and artistic productions. Without the religious pressure from the Puritans, for instance, Burbage would probably never have founded his theatre in Shoreditch in 1576.

The flipside is that many writers have also taken tremendous inspiration from religion. John Donne may have started off writing earthy (and often downright dirty) verses in praise of his lovers, but it was 'three-person'd God' he ultimately wanted to 'batter' his heart. Donne even became Dean of St Paul's and had a benefice in the church of St Dunstan on Fleet Street between 1624 and 1631. In 1620 he also laid the foundation stone of the nearby Lincoln's Inn chapel. It was the bell of this church that inspired his famous lines demanding that we ask not 'for whom the bell tolls' – the bell in question was rung at noon, whenever a member of Lincoln's Inn had died. (It still is, so if you're passing and you hear a clanging, you'll know that a lawyer has left the world.)

'And you, London, a city built by Trojan settlers, a city whose towery head can be seen for miles, you are more than fortunate for you enclose within your walls whatever beauty is to be found in all this pendent world.'

John Milton

John Milton (1608–74) dedicated many of his most famous poems to God – even if the Devil got most of the best lines. He wrote the epic *Paradise Lost* while living on Jewin Street (in a house destroyed in the Second World War, and now under the Barbican site), and during his long life took plenty of other residences in London. Alas, if you hope to find Milton links on Milton Street in Clerkenwell, you are liable to be disappointed. The street isn't named after the poet; rather, it's dedicated to a wealthy 1830s landlord who owned most of the properties in the area. But this is still a place of rich associations. Before the name change it was Grub Street, famous for the number of writers who lived and worked there – and memorialized by Alexander Pope (1688–1744) in *The Dunciad* as a road where 'pensive poets painful vigil keep/Sleepless themselves, to give their readers sleep.' You can find one of Milton's old addresses not far away at 125 Bunhill Row.

'Bunhill' has further religious associations. John Bunyan (1628–88) is buried in Bunhill Fields in Islington (Blake and Defoe lie nearby). The Baptist preacher and religious poet ended up there after his progress was halted on the way into London in August 1688.

Another visiting preacher was Laurence Sterne (1713–68), author of the cheeky – and frankly irreverent – *The Life and Opinions of Tristram Shandy*. Sterne was an Anglican vicar in Coxwold, Yorkshire, but often travelled to London. He met Samuel Johnson in Joshua Reynolds's studio in Soho – at 47 Leicester Square – some time around the publication of the first volume of his novel in 1759. He read the lexicographer the first line of the dedication of *Tristram Shandy*, but Johnson wasn't impressed: 'I told him it was not English, sir,' he later recounted. Like Bunyan, Sterne also ended his days in London. He died in a house at 41 Old Bond Street in 1768, where he had been living for over a year, in dire poverty. As he breathed his last, bailiffs were rifling through his possessions. He was buried in St George's Field (off Bayswater Road, near the present site of Marble Arch), but within days his corpse was stolen by an anatomy professor. According to the Shakespeare scholar Edmond Malone (1741–1812), 'a gentleman who was present at the dissection . . . recognised Sterne's face the moment he saw the body'. The corpse was discreetly buried again, but only achieved full and lasting peace in 1968, when he was once more dug up and returned to Shandy Hall in Coxwold.

London's other great poet priest was Gerard Manley Hopkins (1844–89), who was born in Stratford in east London. In 1854, aged ten, he was packed off to Highgate School, on North Road in Highgate. There he began to take a great interest in early Christian ascetics and bet a friend that he could last longer than him without drinking any water. After a few days, he won – but his tongue turned black and he collapsed. He also won the school poetry competition for 'The Escorial', a poem part-inspired by an earlier resident of his neighbourhood, Keats (and which also obsessed over monks and relics). Later he became a Jesuit, teaching at Maresa House in Roehampton, south London, and he ended up as curate of Farm Street Church in Mayfair.

Among the most pugilistic adherents of the faith to follow Hopkins was Hilaire Belloc (1870–1953), who wrote fierce attacks on scientifically minded rationalists like H. G. Wells (1866–1946) from his rooms in 104 Cheyne Walk, prompting Wells to complain: 'He is the sort of man who talks loud and fast for fear of hearing the other side.'

In Daniel Defoe's *A Journal of the Plague Year* (1722), a religious enthusiast by the name of Solomon Eagles likes to parade about the streets off the Fleet, denouncing the sins of the city ('sometimes quite naked, and with a Pan of burning Charcoal on his Head').

Belloc also wrote a few diatribes while working on the *Morning Post* on Fleet Street – but was sacked for disobedience and failing to keep regular hours. This was because, as well as religion, Belloc enjoyed a drink. One of his most celebrated statements came in the 1930s, during a Saintsbury Club literary dinner at the Vintners' Hall on Thames Street. There he drank a bottle of 1878 Latour, rose to make a speech – and shouted: 'This is wine, I am drunk.' Then he sat down again.

In spite of his eccentricity, Belloc forged strong friendships. He was so close to G. K. Chesterton (1874–1936) that the two men were known collectively as The Chesterbelloc. Chesterton's most famous character was Father Brown, the Catholic priest who found his true calling when he moved from Cobhole in Essex to a life of crime-solving in London. Chesterton himself lived at 11 Warwick Gardens in Kensington, but was often to be seen hunched over a table in El Vino's in Fleet Street, his preferred place for 'hard-drinking and hard-thinking'. (At El Vino's he was renowned less for his religion than for seeing off anyone he didn't like the look of with a Victorian swordstick.)

Less amusingly, Belloc and Chesterton were frequently accused of anti-Semitism, making the fact that they were part of a slowly dying breed more cause for relief than lamentation.

Yet there were still plenty of fine writers who clung to their religion, especially to the romantic Catholicism espoused by London-based novelists like Evelyn Waugh (1903–66) and Graham Greene (1904–91). Waugh converted to Catholicism at the very church in Farm Street in Mayfair where Gerard Manley Hopkins had worked.

The Fleet Street papers were scandalized. 'Young Satirist of Mayfair Turns To Rome' proclaimed the *Daily Express*. 'Ultramodernist Becomes Ultramontanist' ran another.

By this time, Greene had already converted (he was received into the Church in Nottingham in 1926, by a man he described as looking like a character from 'the wrong side of Piccadilly'). In spite of this sincere conversion, Greene's relationship with the Church was problematic. He sometimes described himself as a 'Catholic atheist', and even when he tried to write about faith he sent out mixed signals. *The Power and the Glory* almost found its way onto the Catholic Index (a list of books thought by the Church to be heretical, anti-clerical, lascivious, or a fun mix of all three – and consequently prohibited), and Greene himself received a letter from the Archbishop of Westminster condemning the novel as 'paradoxical' and 'dealing with extraordinary circumstances'. Over in the Vatican, the reader charged with assessing the novel pronounced it as 'Troubling the spirit of calm that should prevail in a Christian'. He also claimed that Greene, as a writer, had 'an abnormal propensity towards . . . sexual immorality'.

They might have said the same of Muriel Spark (1918–2006), described in the *New Yorker* as a 'chronicler of creepy nuns and schoolgirl intrigue', but another pious convert to Catholicism. She turned to the faith in the 1950s while living in a bedsit in Camberwell. Waugh and Greene together helped persuade Macmillan to publish the brilliant debut novel she wrote about this experience – *The Comforters* – even

After his conversion in 1927, T. S. Eliot (1888–1965) began serving as a churchwarden at St Stephen's Church in Kensington – much to the alarm of his Bloomsbury pals. 'Tom Eliot may be called dead to us all from this day forward,' Virginia Woolf declared to a friend. 'He has become an Anglo-Catholic believer in God and immortality.' Eliot stuck to his guns, however, and, despite almost constant needling from Virginia and others, he attended the same church for over thirty years.

On 13 August 1938, the *Guardian* reported that: 'Mr HG Wells' "Short History of the World" was ceremoniously committed to the flames by a party of Indian Mohammedans in the East End.'

The *Guardian* also reported that once the copies of the book had been destroyed, a 1,000-strong delegation from the Jamiat-ul-Muslimin organization were due to make their way to the India Office 'to demand that the book should be somehow or other "proscribed"'.

The outraged mob also threatened to march on Wells's house near Regent's Park – although this doesn't appear to have happened, and the protesters contented themselves instead with a noisy rally, on 19 August, at the Aldwych office of Sir Firoz Khan Noon (High Commissioner for India).

There, marchers chanted 'Down with ignorant Wells' and 'Allah is great'. After their leaders handed over a 'written representation', which the commissioner said he would hand on to the government, a spokesman told a reporter: 'Now we are satisfied.' And that seems to have been the end of that – until Salman Rushdie wrote *The Satanic Verses* in the 1980s.

though Greene told Spark in a letter that the publisher might not be the ideal firm to put out something so 'weird'.

Since Spark, there have been fewer public assumptions of faith. It's also worth noting that the inherent rebelliousness and curious intelligence of writers have led many of them, from Percy Shelley (1792–1822) onwards, to publicly renounce religion. Yet for most of London's history, the Church has managed to get the writers in the end. The very best place to see a large quantity of them (or at least, their remains) is Poets' Corner in Westminster Abbey. There, among others, and alongside numerous monuments and memorials to writers buried elsewhere, you can find the remains of John Gay (1685–1732), Henry James (1843–1916), Rudyard Kipling (1865–1936), Geoffrey Chaucer, Charles Dickens (1812–78 – even though he wanted to be buried in

Rochester), Edmund Spenser (1552–99), John Dryden (1631–1700), Alfred, Lord Tennyson (1809–92), Thomas Hardy (1840–1928 – his body was buried in the Abbey, but his heart was taken in a biscuit tin to the church of St Michael's Stinsford in Dorset), Samuel Johnson (1709–84) and Ben Jonson (1572–1637). The latter is buried upright because he told the Dean at the time: 'Sir, six feet long by two feet wide is too much for me: two feet by two feet will do for all I want.'

KEY ADDRESSES

St Paul's Cathedral, St Paul's Churchyard, EC4M (Tube station: St Paul's)
St Dunstan in the West, Fleet Street, EC4A (Tube station: Chancery Lane, Temple)
Lincoln's Inn Chapel, Treasury Office, WC2A (Tube station: Chancery Lane)
Bunhill Fields, 38 City Road, EC1Y (Tube station: Old Street)
Westminster Abbey, 20 Dean's Yard, London SW1P (Tube station: St James's Park, Westminster)

RECOMMENDED READING

John Donne, *Poems*
Graham Greene, *The End of the Affair*
John Milton, *Paradise Lost*
Evelyn Waugh, *A Handful of Dust*; *Brideshead Revisited*

CHAPTER FOUR

MYSTICS AND MAGICIANS

—ᴍᴍ—

Writers create new lives, peer into the past and the future, make bids for their own immortality and weave strange magic around their readers. It's unsurprising that many of them have had mystical, as well as religious, inclinations and obsessions. Plenty of London figures have taken things that little bit further, however, and started seeing as many things in the aether as they do on the page.

One of the most curious figures is John Dee (1527–1608), the mysterious magician in the Court of Queen Elizabeth I, who advised the monarch on matters astrological and even chose the date for her coronation: 15 January 1559.

Before this, Dee had suffered a few years of exile. He had retired from the capital in 1553 after Mary I accused him of trying to kill her 'by magic' (she threw him into prison for a short period at Hampton Court). Upon his return, Dee set up base at Mortlake near Richmond in south-west London, where he amassed what was to become known as the largest library in Europe. He also managed to write forty-nine books of his own. Most of these tomes were strange and complicated. In 1564, for instance, he wrote *Monas Hieroglyphica*, a book about a 'glyph', a symbol he had drawn to explain the mystical unity of all creation (and which has baffled its few readers ever since). More comprehensible is *General and Rare Memorials Pertayning to the Perfect Arte of Navigation*, a work that set out his vision of a maritime empire and asserted English territorial claims on the New World. This idea caught on – as history shows – but Dee didn't see the rewards. By the time he died in 1609, Elizabeth was gone and he had fallen back out of favour at Court. He retreated to Mortlake and lived there in poverty and obscurity, selling off his treasured books to survive.

Dee was buried in the local graveyard of St Mary the Virgin, but there's no gravestone to mark his final resting place. His house, too, has long since disappeared, and all that remains of it is a garden wall that separates the churchyard from a block of modern flats – called 'John Dee House' in tribute.

As befits a serious mystic, Dee's afterlife has been quite as vivid as his time on earth. There's some evidence that he was the model for Prospero in *The Tempest*, and he also gave James Bond his code number, 007. (Fleming was reading a memoir about Dee when he started writing *Casino Royale*, which explained that Elizabeth referred to Dee as '007' when communicating with him on paper.) Since then, Dee has appeared in numerous novels, among them Michael Scott's *The Secrets of the Immortal Nicholas Flamel*, John Crowley's *Ægypt*, and Peter Ackroyd's *The House of Doctor Dee*, which places the titular house in Cloak Lane in Clerkenwell.

One of Dee's biggest obsessions in his final years was communing with angels and demons, in order to learn the universal language of creation. He didn't succeed in getting the lingo down, but the idea endured. In 1743, for instance, Emmanuel Swedenborg (1688–1772) was dining in a private room at a tavern just around the corner from his lodgings in Salisbury Court, off Fleet Street. At some point during the course of his meal, he noticed that the room was filling up with frogs and snakes – and also that another diner had appeared: a fellow gentleman, who sternly told him to stop eating so much. Swedenborg hurried home, where the man appeared again – announcing that he was, in fact, Jesus. It was at that point that Swedenborg turned from science (in his native Sweden he was a renowned engineer) to writing immense multi-volume works about the conversations he held with winged celestials.

Swedenborg's books in turn inspired a young man called William

London's Ghost Club grew out of the Cambridge gatherings presided over by M. R. James (author of supernatural classics like 'Oh, Whistle, and I'll Come to You, My Lad') before relocating to the capital – where, over suppers at the Maison Jules Restaurant on Jermyn Street, Mayfair, club members such as Arthur Conan Doyle, Charles Dickens, W. B. Yeats, Algernon Blackwood and Siegfried Sassoon held earnest discussions about psychic phenomena. The club is still going today, with monthly meetings in London pubs. (On 2 November every year, the names of all members – living and dead – are recited, and once you've joined it doesn't matter if you die: you're still a member of the club. Dead members are simply marked as non-attending.)

Blake (1757–1827). Blake was born on 28 November 1757 at 28 Broad Street (now Broadwick Street) in Soho – and was, from infancy, immersed in the rich dissenting religion of the area. Clearly a natural rebel himself, he showed such scant regard for discipline at home that his parents packed him off – first to Pars's drawing school on the Strand, then to a seven-year apprenticeship on Great Queen Street with the engraver James Basire. It was after leaving Basire to study at the Royal Academy that Blake developed the Swedenborgian habit of not just seeing, but actively engaging with his visions. He took to talking with angels – as well as sitting naked in his garden in Hercules Road in Lambeth, with his wife, reciting passages from *Paradise Lost*. Whenever people visited, he would invite them to 'come and meet Adam and Eve'.

I wander thro' each charter'd street,
Near where the charter'd Thames does flow.
And mark in every face I meet
Marks of weakness, marks of woe.

William Blake, 'London'

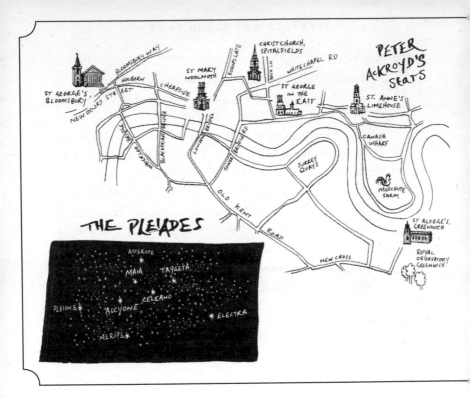

THE PLEIADES

Blake also lived briefly in 17 South Molton Street, where he wrote and illustrated poetry inspired by his visions and angelic communications. Some of these were shown to George II – who wasn't impressed, and asked for them to be taken away immediately. In 1809, Blake held his one and only exhibition above his brother's hosiery shop in Soho's Broad Street. It was reviewed in the *Examiner* by the critic Robert Hunt, who seemed to take the same view as the king. He concluded that the paintings could only be 'the outpourings of a madman', and that the artist was 'an unfortunate lunatic ... suffering egregious vanity'. Not one of the works sold. Posterity has been more kind – and should you wish to commune with Blake yourself, you can see his bust in Westminster Abbey, visit the William Blake estate in Hercules Road, or take a look at the only remaining of his eight London houses, at South Molton Street. You can also see some of the original drafts of Blake's poem 'London' at the British Library in King's Cross.

Peter Ackroyd repeats the trick he perfected in *The House of Doctor Dee* in his other mystical exploration of London's architecture, *Hawksmoor*, where he merges fiction, mysticism and bricks and mortar with fantastic results.

He follows Nicolas Dyer (a character modelled on the real London architect Nicholas Hawksmoor), a member of an underground sect, the Enthusiasticks, who commits sacrifices as part of the construction of churches around London. Dyer views the churches as forming the part of a huge talisman, arranged in a pattern imitating the Pleiades star cluster . . . and, yes, they actually form the shape. Take a look at Christ Church, Spitalfields, St George's, Bloomsbury, St Mary Woolnoth, St George in the East, St Anne's Limehouse, and St Alfege Church, Greenwich on this map.

The churches are all also very beautiful – and well worth a visit – although digging into the foundations to hunt for corpses is currently frowned upon. Bear in mind that Ackroyd's seventh church, Little St Hugh, is a fictional embellishment and thus won't be found by even the most dedicated of readers.

Later in the nineteenth century, John Dee also directly influenced an organization called the Hermetic Order of the Golden Dawn – which, among other things, attempted to channel the god Hermes in the temple it founded in Mark Masons' Hall on 86 St James's Street, in 1888. These days an innocuous-looking venue, back then the Hall was the centre of London's underground 'magick' scene. One of the most famous regulars in the secret rites of the Golden Dawn at the London Lodge was the poet W. B. Yeats (1865–1939), who lived nearby, in Bloomsbury's 5 Euston Square, and used to alarm his neighbours by walking up and down the neighbouring streets, swinging his arms madly. This was his preferred action for communing with the muses – and he dreamed up some of his most famous poetry while so engaged, including his collections *The Green Helmet* and *The Wind among the Reeds*. (No. 5 Euston Square is also significant for Yeats's admirers because when he left in 1917, his great love Maud Gonne moved in.)

Also initiated into the Golden Dawn at Mark Masons' Hall was one Aleister Crowley (1875–1947). The Order promised a gruesome death to those who shared its secrets, but Crowley (author of such famous magic books as the *Book of Lies*, as well as the startling *Diary of a Drug Fiend*) not only cheerfully told all and sundry about the rituals, he also stole them, and set up his own cult at his luxurious flat at 67–69 Chancery Lane. Crowley fitted this flat out as a temple; one room was full of mirrors and another contained a human skeleton that Crowley fed with blood and dead sparrows. In this lair, he took voluminous quantities of drugs and attempted to summon demons – right up until the day in 1889 when, inspired to move to Boleskine in Scotland, he passed on from London.

The remorseless march of science and reason made angelic visitations an increasing rarity, but there was one last grand fling of spiritualism at the end of the nineteenth century and in the first decades of the twentieth – especially following the horrors of the First World War. One of the most tragic stories relates to Arthur Conan Doyle (1859–1930), who became increasingly interested in the other side after the death of his son Kingsley, towards the end of the war. Conan Doyle joined the Spiritualists National Union and took to attending séances around the capital, including those at the Bloomsbury home of the magician P. T. Selbit. Despite many of these spiritualists later being debunked as frauds – and even in some cases admitting to trickery themselves – Conan Doyle refused to believe anything against them. He needed the afterlife too much by then, and was so serious about spiritualism that he wrote a novella on the matter, *The Land of Mist*. He also asked that, after his own death, a séance should be held. In it, he said, he would come back – and in glorious fashion prove all the doubters wrong. Accordingly, in July 1930, shortly after he died, a gathering was arranged at the Royal Albert Hall. An empty chair was set up for him, with a card on top of it reading 'Sir Arthur Conan Doyle'. Alas, no one saw him sit in it.

By 1900 the Golden Dawn had moved from its more central location on St James's Street to 36 Blythe Road, Kensington. Here, on 9 April, Aleister Crowley and W. B. Yeats had a 'magical battle'. This kicked off when an exuberant Crowley, wearing a black mask, burst into the offices of the Order, shouting that he was going to take over the sect. He then proceeded to shower those present with incantations and hexes – and all no doubt would have been lost if it hadn't been for Yeats, who also happened to be in the building and had a few counter-spells of his own. These were powerful enough to hold Crowley off until the Metropolitan Police Constabulary arrived, but any triumph Yeats felt was short-lived. Crowley was quickly and officially forgiven by the head of the Golden Dawn, Yeats himself was expelled – and he also spent several years in fear of Crowley, who busied himself carving wax figures of the poet, to stick pins in. He also (or so Yeats was convinced) hired a local Lambeth gang, paying them a retainer of eight shillings a day, to 'grievously maim or preferably slaughter' the poet.

KEY ADDRESSES

Royal Academy, Burlington House, Piccadilly, W1J (Tube station: Piccadilly)

17 South Molton Street, London, W1 (Tube station: Bond Street)

British Library, 96 Euston Road, NW1 (Tube station: King's Cross)

Mark Masons' Hall, 86 St James's Street, SW1A (Tube station: Piccadilly)

Royal Albert Hall, Kensington Gore, SW7 (Tube station: South Kensington)

RECOMMENDED READING

Peter Ackroyd, *The House of Doctor Dee*; *Hawksmoor*; *Blake*

William Blake, *The Complete Illuminated Works*; *Songs of Experience*

William Butler Yeats, *Autobiography*

CHAPTER FIVE
DIARISTS AND LEXICOGRAPHERS

—⚉—

N o book like this one would be complete without due reference to Dr Samuel Johnson's famous remark: 'When a man is tired of London he is tired of life.'

Johnson knew that the capital isn't just a fine place to be a writer – it was also a good subject for writing. So good that many of the finest books about London aren't fictional at all. There's no need to make things up when there's so much going on around you – and London boasts a correspondingly rich tribe of diarists, lexicographers, memoirists and psychogeographers.

One of the first among them was the boy king Edward VI (1537– 53), the son of Henry VIII (1491–1547). Edward started keeping a diary while also sitting on the throne of England, aged just thirteen. Although often concerned with state visits to Hampton Court palace, Edward also wrote about events in the city nearby. He visited bear-baiting shows and noted when there were riots about the 'unreasonable prices of thinges'. On 10 July 1551, he also recorded: 'At this time came the sweat into London, which was more vehement then the old sweat. For if one took cold he died within 3 houres, and if he escaped it held him but 9 houres, or 10 at the most.' Edward dodged the sweating sickness, but his diary is still short. He completed just sixty-eight leaves of writing (which can be seen in the British Library near St Pancras) before he died, aged fifteen, in 1552 – some say of TB, others from drinking poison.

By the time of Edward's demise, diaries were becoming more

popular. One diarist, an undertaker called Henry Machyn (1498–1563), was even present at the young monarch's funeral at Westminster Abbey, recording: 'And at his burying was the greatest moan made for him of his death as ever was heard or seen.'

Machyn, who began his diary in 1550, went on to describe numerous trials, hangings and events around the city, including the first description we have of the Lord Mayor's Show and a glimpse of Elizabeth I's coronation, when Machyn said all the city 'made merry' as they watched the Queen process down Cheapside from the Tower, surrounded by courtiers clad in red velvet.

Also not to be forgotten is John Stow (1524–1605), who mapped Elizabethan London in his 1598 *Survey of London* – and included, as well as the tavern and street names, some entertainingly colourful descriptions of the local life, including piratical raids on the city's docks and ports. But the earliest diary most people still read for pleasure belongs, of course, to Samuel Pepys (1633–1703). Pepys's diary endures partly because he lived in such interesting times, working at the heart of government during the Restoration of Charles II and the controversial reign of James II. But it's also just a delight, because Pepys (who wrote in code and thought his diaries would never be seen) is so unfiltered and exuberant in his commentary on London life.

Most famously, he witnessed the horrors of the Plague and the ravages of the Great Fire of London on 2 September 1666. He saw the early stages of the fire from his window in Seething Lane, near Tower Hill, but at first thought little of it, to the point that he actually went back to sleep.

He wasn't alone in this casual assessment. The mayor of London (Sir Thomas Bloodworth, 1620–82) saw the same flames and declared, 'Pish! A woman might piss it out!' Within three days, 400 acres of buildings were destroyed – and Pepys's subsequent account of the 'infinite fury' of the fire is justly famous.

Pepys was just as eloquent on more trivial matters. On 1 July 1663 he tells of an evening in the inevitably named Cock Tavern in Bow Street (also a favoured haunt of the libertine Lord Rochester (1647–80)), during which the poet and dramatist Sir Charles Sedley (1639–1701) and the poet and courtier Lord Buckhurst (1638–1706) showed off their manhoods – the former apparently dipping his into a glass of wine and then downing the contents while toasting the king.

'[I hurried] to [St] Paul's; and there walked along Watling Street, as well as I could, every creature coming away laden with goods to save and, here and there, sick people carried away in beds. Extraordinary goods carried in carts and on backs. At last [I] met my Lord Mayor in Cannon Street, like a man spent, with a [handkerchief] about his neck. To the King's message he cried, like a fainting woman, "Lord, what can I do? I am spent: people will not obey me. I have been pulling down houses, but the fire overtakes us faster than we can do it."'

Samuel Pepys, *Diary*

Pepys himself also indulged in bad behaviour. One of the naughtiest episodes in the diary takes place in St Dunstan's Church in Fleet Street, where he says he 'did labour' to take 'a pretty maid' by hand and 'by body' during a sermon. Fortunately, she repelled his amours with some pins she had in her pocket.

If you're ever on Bankside, head to the Anchor at 34 Park Street. As well as laying good claim to being one of Shakespeare's locals, and one of the places from which Pepys watched the Great Fire of London, Johnson wrote a sizeable portion of his *Dictionary* in a private room in the pub – which, at the time, was owned by his friend Henry Thrale.

A century or so after Pepys, a young Scotsman was just as keen to get to know the female population of London. James Boswell arrived in town in 1762, and soon after recorded in his diary: 'It is very curious to think that I have now been in London several weeks without ever enjoying the delightful sex, although I am surrounded with numbers of free-hearted ladies of all kinds.'

These words were lost until the 1920s, when they were rediscovered in a Dublin castle – and scholars were astonished to find them among numerous other stories about engaging prostitutes on the 'noble edifice' of Westminster Bridge and there meeting 'signor gonorrhea'.

This dangerous gentleman was not the only notable person Boswell met in London. On 16 May 1763 he first encountered the poet, lexicographer and wit Samuel Johnson in Davies's Bookshop, 8 Russell Street. Things did not get off to a great start. According to legend, Boswell opened with, 'I come from Scotland but I cannot help it.' To which Johnson replied, 'That I find is what a great many of your countrymen cannot help.'

Even so, the two hit it off. Boswell became a regular at Johnson's house at 1 Inner Temple Lane (Johnson had moved here not long before, after leaving his other address – now a museum to his life – at 17 Gough Square). He noted admiringly: 'Johnson lives in a very literary state, very solemn and very slovenly.'

For the next twenty-one years that he knew Johnson, Boswell remained an assiduous journal-keeper – and the entries he made went on to form the basis for his famous biography of the great man, which was published in 1791 to lasting acclaim. In spite of this success, Boswell struggled in his final years. A year before publishing his life of Johnson, he had been thrown into jail for making a racket while drunk near his current house at 122 Great Portland Street. His defence was that he had been trying to teach the nightwatchman the time. He also suffered from venereal disease, and most of those he had written about were dead – as was his wife. In spite of his earlier opposition to enforced labour, his last published work before his death in 1795 was a poem about a 'cheerful gang' of slaves enjoying their work.

'Sir, if you wish to have a just notion of the magnitude of this city, you must not be satisfied with seeing its great streets and squares, but must survey the innumerable little lanes and courts. It is not in the showy revolutions of buildings, but in the multiplicity of human habitations which are crowded together, that the wonderful immensity of London consists.'

Samuel Johnson, quoted in Boswell's *Life*

John Evelyn (1620–1706) was a diarist contemporary to Pepys. He lived in Deptford for most of his adult life, at Sayes Court – just up the road from where Marlowe was killed (see p.13). He wrote many volumes of journals covering key incidents of seventeenth- century London life, from outbreaks of plague to the Great Fire of London – and also created a celebrated garden that thousands of people flocked to see. This garden survived until the twentieth century only to be destroyed by the twin evils of the Second World War and town planning. This destruction was a key inspiration to the formation of the National Trust.

Evelyn actually wasn't all that fond of London. 'Cough and consumption range more on this one City,' he wrote, 'than in the whole Earth besides.'

He was also *much* better behaved than Samuel Pepys – which might explain why he isn't as well remembered.

A later celebrity diarist was not so keen on getting into trouble on Westminster Bridge. Queen Victoria (1819–1901) kept a journal for most of her sixty-year reign, completing over 100 manuscript volumes by the time of her death. These are rarely read because, frankly, most of them are dull. But there are some fascinating titbits, about the queen's family life, her fears of illness among her relations, her daily routines, her displeasure at the new wave of London suffragists ('mad, wicked folly'). Even better are a few bright highlights such as her

JOHNSON'S DEFINITIONS

Dull: Not exhilaterating [*sic*]; not delightful; as, *to make dictionaries is dull work.*

Kickshaw: A dish so changed by the cookery that it can scarcely be known.

Lexicographer: A writer of dictionaries; a harmless drudge that busies himself in tracing the original, and detailing the signification of words.

Oats: A grain, which in England is generally given to horses, but in Scotland supports the people.

Patron: One who countenances, supports or protects. Commonly a wretch who supports with insolence, and is paid with flattery.

To worm: To deprive a dog of something, nobody knows what, under his tongue, which is said to prevent him, nobody knows why, from running mad.

account of her coronation and of visiting the Great Exhibition at Crystal Palace. Alas, there are also endless observations about the weather.

In sharp contrast to Victoria's long prosperous life was the tragically short one of Bruce Frederick Cummings (1889–1919). This all-too-young Londoner took the pen-name Wilhelm Nero Pilate Barbellion after discovering that he had multiple sclerosis, and deciding to publish what would become one of the greatest London diaries of all: *The Journal of a Disappointed Man.*

Barbellion found out about his illness in the early days of the First World War, when he was turned away from a recruiting office as unfit to serve. He got a job at the Natural History Museum, noting, with typical suavity: 'Of course I am wonderfully proud of being at the Museum, although I am disappointed and write as if I were quite blasé.' He kept working and writing – with wit, humour and heart-breaking candour about his physical decline – until his death aged thirty in 1919. His last entry read 'self-disgust'. Generations of readers have felt the very opposite emotion towards him.

> **'When I am dead, you can boil me, burn me, drown me, scatter me – but you cannot destroy me: my little atoms would merely deride such heavy vengeance. Death can do no more than kill you.'**
>
> Barbellion

Also on the home front in the First World War were a number of fine female diarists. Hallie Miles (c.1868–1948) recorded the events of the first Blitz in 1915 (and also interesting material about running a pioneering vegetarian restaurant on Chandos Place near Covent Garden, popular with the local bohemians, and also thanks to meat-rationing restrictions) in *Untold Tales of Wartime London*. Meanwhile, Vera Brittain (1893–1970) was working at the 1st London General Hospital in Camberwell and recording the journal entries that would later be published as *Chronicle of Youth* – and that formed the basis for her lament for a lost generation, *Testament of Youth*.

During the same war, Virginia Woolf began her long and troubled journal. Her first entry was made on 1 January 1915, when she was living in Richmond and the legend of the Bloomsbury Set was well under way. One of her entries in March 1920 begins with a salutation to her future, older, self: 'Greetings! my dear ghost; and take heed that I don't think 50 a very great age.' Tragic words, for a woman who took her own life during the Second World War at the age of fifty-nine.

After the Second World War diarists sprouted all over London. Among them, the politician Tony Benn (1925–2014) published volume after volume meticulously recording speeches made, arguments won and lost and pipes smoked. Meanwhile, in Farley Court off Marylebone Road, Kenneth Williams (1926–88) recorded the bitter, tragic thoughts – and acidic commentaries on his fellow actors – which shocked the world after his death.

The post-war years also saw a rich vein of new writing about London from writers like Iain Sinclair (1943–), Roy Porter (1946–2002), Peter Ackroyd (1949–) and Will Self (1961–), who have made walking though the city and uncovering its many layers of history an art form in itself. Iain Sinclair even tramped around the M25 in *London Orbital*, symbolically ringing the city in his peregrination, occasionally breaking to chow down on all-day breakfasts in supermarket cafés.

More straightforward, but equally delightful, are the diaries of Alan Bennett (1934–), which he has kept for many years in the various homes he's occupied in London. His address in Camden Town (23 Gloucester Crescent) has become famous. While he lived there between 1974 and 1989, a woman known as 'Miss Shepherd' stayed on his drive in her van. This became the subject of a play he wrote – *The Lady in the Van* – and a 2016 film. When the latter was made, the Camden house was used, with an old van parked outside as part of the film set. One night it was 'used' by a passing couple. The next morning it had to be deep-cleaned – and then filthied up again to create the right look for Miss Shepherd's home. It seems that Pepys and Boswell weren't the only ones …

KEY ADDRESSES

Faryners House, Pudding Lane, EC1 (Tube station: Monument)
Doctor Johnson's House, 17 Gough Square, EC4A (Tube station: Chancery Lane)
Boswell's House, 122 Great Portland Street, W1W (Tube station: Warren Street)

RECOMMENDED READING

Peter Ackroyd, *London*
W. N. P. Barbellion, *The Journal of a Disappointed Man*
James Boswell, *The Life of Samuel Johnson*
Hallie Miles, *Untold Tales of Wartime London*
Roy Porter, *London: A Social History*

CHAPTER SIX

GOSSIPS AND RIVALS

—⅏—

London has nurtured many fond literary friendships. It has brought hundreds of writers together, huddling in cafés, plotting over cheap wine, dreaming up new movements, writing manifestos . . . It has been the gathering place for countless schools, counter-schools and new paradigms. It has seen endless -isms. It has been the central node for pre-, post-, ante-post- and new pre-post versions of most of those -isms. It's even given performance poets a safe place to practise their dread art.

There's a lot to be said for such harmony and the free exchange of ideas. And there's also a lot to be said for the direct opposite. Literary rivalry has an equally important place – and has spurred writers on for centuries in London, adding venom to their ink, urgency to their writing, and producing a slew of fine invective.

Naturally, many of the best stories about squabbling writers in the capital city centre upon the duelling and disputatious Elizabethans. Next time you hear someone waxing lyrical about Shakespeare, spare a thought for Robert Greene (1558–92). This jealous man was so annoyed at his fellow playwright and neighbour's early success that, in a pamphlet written in 1592, he called him an 'upstart crow, beautified with our feathers'. And he didn't stop there:

> [He] supposes he is as well able to bombast out a blanke verse as the best of you: and being an absolute *Iohannes fac totum*, is in his owne conceit the only Shake-scene in a countrey.

A *'Iohannes fac totum'* is a Jack-of-all-trades, master of none. Ouch!

Sadly this rivalry was cut short – and Shakespeare didn't get a chance to reply – because Greene died before his pamphlet was published. He'd suffered, according to the scholar Gabriel Harvey (1552–1631), from 'a surfeit of pickle herring and Rhenish wine' and is buried in the Bedlam churchyard in Bromley. Perhaps it's as well that Shakespeare didn't have to respond.

In 1598, Ben Jonson (who was always up for a fight, as we saw in this book's first chapter) was so incensed at a fellow actor, Gabriel Spencer (1578–98), that he fought a duel with him in Hoxton (then called 'Hogsden') Fields. Gabriel died. Ben Jonson only survived by claiming right of clergy – a legal feint whereby he recited a Bible verse in order to escape execution. He did have to give up everything he owned, though, and his right thumb was branded.

Just under a hundred years later, John Wilmot, Earl of Rochester (1647–80) also started causing trouble. Few writers have dedicated themselves quite so assiduously to annoying their fellow men, or managed it quite so effectively. In his *Allusion to Horace*, he managed to insult just about every other poet and playwright in London, accusing them of being 'obscene', 'hasty' and 'slow', and of imparting 'none of art'. He singled out for particular attention the poet laureate at the time, John Dryden:

> *Well Sir, 'tis granted, I said Dryden's Rhimes,*
> *Were stoln, unequal, nay dull many times:*
> *What foolish Patron, is there found of his,*
> *So blindly partial, to deny me this?*

Later on in the poem he also called Dryden the 'Poet Squab', suggested he was impotent, and made jokes so bawdy that we fear to reprint them here, nearly 400 years after their first creation.

These insults must have stung, especially because the two men had once been friends. Even though Dryden was prone to writing long plays about virtue, he and Rochester – a man as well known for his rampant sexual proclivities as for his plays – initially hit it off. Rochester even helped Dryden with some dialogue in his play *Marriage-à-la-mode* (apparently by adding jokes about premature ejaculation). But things quickly soured. When he was told that Dryden had written a new play in three weeks, Rochester snorted: 'Three weeks? How the devil could he have been so long about it?' Then Rochester took to insulting him in verse, and told everyone that Dryden was gunning for him, too. In 1678 he took it into his head that Dryden had libelled him in an anonymously published 'essay upon satire', which called Rochester 'mean in each action, lewd in every limb'.

Of all the stories about Rochester (and there are many), perhaps one of the best concerns the time when, after yet another street fight in 1676, Rochester – fearful of what the king might do – hid out in the precincts of Tower Hill. There he set up shop as 'Doctor Bendo' and advertised his services as a gynecologist. His cure for barrenness – which consisted of offering himself as a sperm donor – was a huge success, and he enjoyed the job so much that he stuck to his disguise for some time.

Most people today believe the essay was actually written by the Earl of Mulgrave (1648–1721), but Rochester was convinced it was his former friend, and was so incensed that he hired three men to rough up the hapless poet laureate. They cornered Dryden outside the Lamb and Flag (a pub you can still visit on Rose Street, near Covent Garden – and which was once known, appropriately enough, as the 'bucket of blood') on a dark December night in 1679 – and there proceeded to beat him senseless with cudgels. Rochester insisted that he wasn't responsible; either way, he certainly rejoiced in the attack, even if it failed to end his rival's career.

It was Dryden who had the last laugh, however. Rochester died of syphilis within a year. Dryden managed another twenty years of productive writing, in the course of which (Bon Jovi fans will be pleased to note) he coined the phrase 'blaze of glory'. Those last decades were not entirely a bed of roses, in spite of these minor triumphs. Dryden fell out of favour after the Glorious Revolution; his laureateship was snatched away, and he moved to poky rooms at 43 Gerrard Street, where he continued scribbling away even when he didn't have the money for food. At this address, he and his wife also annoyed the neighbours by arguing constantly. She saw books as her main rival, and when she once complained that she would have a better relationship with him if she were a book herself, he replied, 'If you do become a book, let it be an almanac, for then I shall change you every year.' (A couple of centuries later the building became the site of the very literary 43 Club, a pre-First World War haunt attended by the likes of Chesterton and Conrad, and where the landlady claimed that the place was watched over by Dryden's jealous ghost.)

Other rivalries may have not been so violent as Dryden's and Rochester's, but they've often been vicious. Lord Byron (1788–1824), who in the early nineteenth century lived in the luxurious 'Albany', a

Sheridan's famous play *The Rivals* was not about literary but rather young love rivals. But it's worth mentioning in this chapter because of events on its opening night at Covent Garden Theatre on 17 January 1775. The audience, who didn't enjoy the play, showed their disapproval by throwing fruit onto the stage. When one actor was hit by an apple, he was prompted to step out of his role and ask: 'By the pow'rs, is it *personal*? – is it me, or the matter?' The audience indicated it was both – so loudly that Sheridan withdrew the play, rewrote it, and cut the role of the actor in question. *The Rivals* went back on stage eleven days later to huge acclaim, has been a mainstay of London theatres ever since – and has even added to the English language, since the term malapropism was coined in reference to the word-muddling character Mistress Malaprop.

group of bachelor apartments just off Piccadilly, had very little time for the lower-born writer John Keats (1795–1821). Keats, he sniped in a letter to his publisher John Murray, wrote 'piss a bed poetry' and verses like 'onanism – something like the pleasure an Italian fiddler extracted out of being suspended daily by a Street Walker in Drury Lane . . .' Keats was more quietly bitchy, writing to his brother: 'There is this great difference between us. [Byron] describes what he sees – I describe what I imagine – Mine is the hardest task.'

Even when Byron heard of Keats's death, he couldn't help sticking the knife in about Keats's 'Cockneyfying and Suburbing' poetry; he also suggested that Keats had burst a blood vessel because of a bad review. (He himself, he said, responded to bad reviews by drinking 'three bottles of claret'.)

'No more Keats, I entreat: flay him alive; if some of you don't I must skin him myself.'

Lord Byron on John Keats

A few decades later in the nineteenth century, Charles Dickens and William Makepeace Thackeray (1811–63) had a brief and unpleasant spat over the breakup of Dickens's marriage in 1858. After Thackeray criticized Dickens over his treatment of his wife, Dickens allowed his friend Edmund Yates (1831–94) to print an attack on the author of *Vanity Fair* in his magazine *Household Words*, drawn from slanderous gossip overheard in the Garrick Club, near Leicester Square. Outraged that the article was based on conversations from the club, Thackeray took the quarrel to the Garrick's committee, who expelled Yates. He in his turn wrote more articles and even wrote a book about the upset: *The Garrick Club, the correspondence and facts.* Meanwhile, Dickens gave up his membership.

'I am become a sort of great man in my way – all but at the top of the tree; indeed there if truth be known and having a great fight up there with Dickens,' wrote Thackeray. Yet while he joked, the argument with his old friend gave him great sadness. Luckily the two men made it up, after meeting by chance on the steps of the Garrick just a few months before Thackeray's death in 1863.

Fighting was not just a male preserve. Shortly after she moved to London in 1894, Elizabeth Robins (1862–1952) dedicated the first few months of her life in the capital to writing a novel, *George Mandeville's Husband*, which lampooned George Eliot, calling Robins's eminent predecessor 'abnormal' and more to be 'pitied than blazoned abroad as example and excuse'.

A few years later, over in Gordon Square in Bloomsbury, Virginia Woolf became so envious of her friend and neighbour Katherine Mansfield (1881–1923) that she began to belittle her in conversation and print: 'Her mind is an inch of soil,' she wrote of Mansfield, 'laid an inch or two upon very barren rock.' She also described her, when she first met her, as like 'a civet cat that had taken to street walking'. Mansfield got her own back by referring to Leonard (1880–1969) and Virginia as 'The Woolves' ('and *smelly* ones, at that') and in October 1920 was less than glowing about Virginia's second novel, *Night and Day*, in the London magazine *The Athenaeum*. By then living on East Heath Street in Hampstead, a mile or two away from Bloomsbury, Mansfield also wrote sneeringly to their mutual London friend and fellow Bloomsberry Ottoline Morrell (1873–1938):

> I see Virginia's book is announced in today's Times Literary Supplement. I expect it will be acclaimed as a masterpiece and she will be drawn around a carriage in Gordon Square in a chariot designed by Roger after a supper given by Clive.

When Mansfield died, however, Virginia was desolate, and said there was no point in writing any more: 'Katherine won't read it, Katherine's my rival no longer.'

Stinging as Woolf and Mansfield could be, the champion feud-monger in the early twentieth century was H. G. Wells (1866–1946). He called his friend and fellow Londoner George Bernard Shaw (1856–1950) 'an idiot child screaming in a hospital', and said of the average sentence by Henry James (1843–1916) that it was 'a delicate creature swathed in relative clauses as an invalid in shawls'.

Henry James gave as good as he got at first, writing an article in the *Times Literary Supplement* in 1914 lumping Wells in with a generation of authors producing 'affluents turbid and unrestrained'. But Wells responded by dedicating a whole chunk of his experimental novel *Boon* to making fun of James and having a 'complimentary' copy delivered to James at the Reform Club on Pall Mall. James was mortified. He wrote a stiff letter to Wells about his bad manners – and died soon afterwards at his home nearby, at 21 Carlyle Mansions, in Chelsea.

That didn't stop Wells from falling out with other friends, however. Later in his life he had an especially fraught relationship with George Orwell (1903–50). For a while he let the younger man stay in a flat above the garage of his house at Hanover Terrace – only to then throw him out on the paranoid grounds that Orwell was gossiping about him. Orwell found new lodgings on Abbey Road in St John's Wood, and asked Wells around for dinner to patch things up. Wells, in turn, wrote back asking Orwell why he had left his flat so suddenly. Orwell's astonishment was increased when Wells arrived, tucked into two helpings of curry and plum cake, and then wrote another letter to Orwell: 'You knew I was ill and on a diet, you deliberately plied me with food and drink. I never want to see you again.' It was the last time Orwell heard from him.

Wells also fell out with D. H. Lawrence (1885–1930) after his one-time protégé wrote a harsh review of his book *The World of William Clissold*. 'This book,' wrote Lawrence, 'is all chewed-up newspaper, and chewed-up scientific reports, like a mouse's nest.' Two years after slaying him in print, Lawrence sent a signed copy of *Lady Chatterley's Lover* to Wells. This wasn't exactly a peace offering. He told a friend that he wondered how stuffy old Wells liked his story of sex and stables. 'It would,' he said, 'amuse me to know.'

Lawrence never found out – but the rest of us have. In May 2002 this very copy went up for sale at an antiquarian book fair. Wells had written on the title page: 'My God what stuff.' He'd also drawn two cartoons. One shows Lawrence with a great big erection, to which he is shouting 'Up Jenkins'. This is captioned 'DHL by himself'. The next shows the author at the foot of an obelisk, looking sadly at a tiny male member. He is asking, 'Well, has any other man the equal of it?' This is captioned: 'The real DHL'.

More forgiving were Edith Sitwell (1887–1964) and her brother Osbert (1892–1969). They engaged in a forty-year feud with Noël Coward (1899–1973) after Coward lampooned them in a West End play called *London Calling!* They appeared as the 'Swiss Family Whittlebot', and Coward sent up Edith's poetry – she is presented as 'Hernia Whittlebot', who breakfasts on onions and Vichy water and is writing a new volume of poetry called *Gilded Sluts*.

The Sitwells were notorious and very self-conscious eccentrics (in Osbert's *Who's Who* entry he described his hobbies as 'regretting the Bourbons, Repartee, and Tu Quoque'). But they finally ended the decades-long fight when Edith invited Coward over for afternoon tea at her flat in Hampstead, where she said she found him 'very sweet'.

KEY ADDRESSES
The Lamb and Flag, Rose Street, WC2E (Tube station: Covent Garden)
The Garrick Club, 15 Garrick Street, WC2E (Tube station: Leicester Square)
Katherine Mansfield's House, 17 East Heath Street, NW3 (Tube station: Hampstead)

RECOMMENDED READING
Lord Rochester, *Collected Poems*
Richard Brinsley Sheridan, *The Rivals*
H. G. Wells, *Boon*

CHAPTER SEVEN

ROMANTICS AND CORPSES

—⚹—

'Hell is a city much like London,' Shelley once wrote:

A populous and a smoky city;
There are all sorts of people undone,
And there is little or no fun done.

Byron was even less complimentary. In *Don Juan*, he described London as:

A mighty mass of brick, and smoke, and shipping,
Dirty and dusty, but as wide as eye
Could reach, with here and there a sail just skipping
In sight, then lost amidst the forestry
Of masts; a wilderness of steeples peeping
On tiptoe through their sea-coal canopy;
A huge, dun cupola, like a foolscap crown
On a fool's head – and there is London Town.

A dunce's cap in other words. Anyone would think that he didn't like the place.

There's also the notable fact that many Romantic poets spent most of their careers extolling the majesty of nature, the comforts of Cumbria, or (for those less inclined to the rural life) the adventures of Spanish Lotharios. Shelley died far away, in the Gulf of Spezia off the north coast of Italy. Keats took his last troubled breath in Rome near the Spanish Steps. Byron expired at Lepanto, in the Gulf of Corinth. Wordsworth died under the clouds of Grasmere.

But it's also worth noting that, even if they treated it with ambivalence, London was always the centre of the Romantic world. Shelley also wrote:

> *You are now*
> *In London, that great sea, whose ebb and flow*
> *At once is deaf and loud, and on the shore*
> *Vomits its wrecks, and still howls on for more.*
> *Yet in its depth what treasures!*

One of those treasures was Thomas Chatterton (1752–70), whose tragic story and small legacy of poems did more than anything else to help create the Romantic sensibility. Thomas was a precocious boy from Bristol who wrote poems from the age of twelve and, when he was seventeen, cancelled his indenture as a lawyer's apprentice and hitched a ride to London (paying his way with donations from friends and acquaintances). His idea was that he would make his name as a poet and political commentator in the city, but in fact he lasted only four months, dying on 24 August 1770 in a garret on Brook Street, near what is now the site of the British Museum. He had taken arsenic. Some say that he was depressed because no one would publish his poems – and his demise was made all the more poignant because when the verses did see the light of day in 1777, they were hailed as masterpieces (even if there was considerable debate about whether they had been written by him or by a fifteenth-century monk called Thomas Rowley, who he had invented himself).

This mystery, this invocation of the past, this story of lost youth, became a foundation myth for a movement including William Wordsworth (1770–1850) and Samuel Taylor Coleridge (1772–1834), and – later – Lord George Gordon Byron, Percy Bysshe Shelley and John Keats. All were 'half in love with easeful death'.

All visited the literary landmarks of the metropolis with the same aspirations as Chatterton. All too, at one point or another, either dedicated or wrote poems commemorating Chatterton, such as Coleridge's 'Monody on the Death of Chatterton', and Keats's sonnet 'To Chatterton'.

So far, so gloomy, and yet these young men also loved to party. Byron particularly was a man about town in London, and guest of honour at numerous grand masquerades at swanky places like Holland House. At one of these he met the aristocratic novelist Caroline Lamb (1785–1828), who became his lover. The pair scandalized high society over the spring and summer of 1812 with a very public affair – and when Byron's affections started to wane, Caroline supplied fuel to the Mayfair gossips with increasingly unstable behaviour. On 8 July, for example, she dressed up as a page and broke into the roguish poet's apartments at 8 St James's Street ('a crowd collected about the door', wrote Byron's friend John Hobhouse), and when Byron stopped returning her letters and refused to elope with her, she dressed her manservants in new livery, with buttons engraved with 'Ne crede Byron' ('Don't believe Byron' – a riff on the family motto 'Crede Byron').

B erry Bros & Rudd's Wine Merchants (3 St James's Street) has had the same slanted floor since 1698 (better for rolling barrels). It was Byron's shop of choice for his wine cellar. He also liked to weigh himself on the shop's enormous coffee scales.

Other Romantics could also be found at private dinners in Soho with notables like the critic and painter William Hazlitt (1778–1830) or another passionate Romantic supporter, the painter Benjamin Haydon (1786–1846).

Haydon, on 28 December 1817, hosted a dinner at 22 Lisson Grove North, Paddington, which included William Wordsworth, the essayist

Charles Lamb (1775–1834 – no relation to Caroline) and the young John Keats.

These days remembered – if at all – for their children's classic *Tales from Shakespeare*, Charles and Mary Lamb (1775–1834 and 1764–1847) were a devoted brother-and-sister writing team who, at the time, were key and popular members of the Romantic set. Charles was described by his biographer E. V. Lucas as 'the most lovable figure in English literature' – although there was a darker side to their biography. Mary struggled with psychotic episodes, and one night in 1796 when Charles was twenty-one, he returned to the family home on Little Queen Street, High Holborn, to find that she had stabbed their mother to death. She was incarcerated in Fisher House in Islington, and Charles saved her from lifelong confinement by agreeing to take responsibility for her and make sure that she was cared for at home. This he did, and – apart from short spells in asylums, whenever Charles or Mary felt that her 'derangement' was returning – the pair lived together, 'in a kind of double singleness', in apartments and houses all over the city. There they held relaxed literary salons ('at homes'), which were attended by Wordsworth, Coleridge and many other Romantics.

'The man must have a rare recipe for melancholy, who can be dull in Fleet Street. I am naturally inclined to hypochondria, but in London it vanishes, like all other ills.'

Charles Lamb

Haydon wrote about this gathering of greats in his autobiography (published posthumously in 1853):

On December 28th the immortal dinner came off in my painting-room, with Jerusalem towering up behind us as a background. Wordsworth was in fine cue, and we had a glorious set-to – on Homer, Shakespeare, Milton and Virgil. Lamb got exceedingly merry and exquisitely witty; and his fun in the midst of Wordsworth's solemn intonations of oratory was like the sarcasm and wit of the fool in the intervals of Lear's passion. He made a speech and voted me absent, and made them drink my health. 'Now,' said Lamb, 'you old lake poet, you rascally poet, why do you call Voltaire dull?'

Luckily, Wordsworth saw the funny side and joined in the laughter. The evening also tickled Keats enough for him also to recount it in a letter to his brother: 'Lamb got tipsy and blew up Kingston, proceeding so far as to take the candle across the room, and show us wh-a-at-sort-fellow he-waas . . .'

Earth has not anything to show more fair:
Dull would he be of soul who could pass by
A sight so touching in its majesty:
This City now doth, like a garment, wear
The beauty of the morning: silent, bare,
Ships, towers, domes, theatres, and temples lie
Open unto the fields, and to the sky;
All bright and glittering in the smokeless air.
Never did sun more beautifully steep
In his first splendour, valley, rock, or hill;
Ne'er saw I, never felt, a calm so deep!
The river glideth at his own sweet will:
Dear God! the very houses seem asleep;
And all that mighty heart is lying still!

William Wordsworth, 'Upon Westminster Bridge'

As well as fun, London also provided the Romantics with plenty of trouble. Shelley, for instance, was once found sleepwalking through

Leicester Square, half a mile from his lodgings in Poland Street.

In his autobiography, the publisher William Jerdan (1782–1869) told a strange story about a man who was found hanged in Hyde Park in 1813. The pockets of his shirt bore the initials S. T. Coleridge, prompting a newspaper to print a story about the poet's suicide, in spite of the recent success of his play *Remorse* – and also causing a man in the coffee room of a London hotel to remark: 'It was very extraordinary that Coleridge the poet should have hanged himself just after the success of his play; but he was always a strange mad fellow.' The man opposite him replied: 'Indeed, sir, it is a *most extraordinary* thing that he should have hanged himself, be the subject of an inquest, and yet that he should at this moment be speaking to you.'

It was the poet himself, who, it transpired, was prone to losing his shirts when he travelled.

Also in Hyde Park, Shelley loved to head down to the Serpentine and skim pebbles and float paper boats – a hobby he'd had since childhood. But his pleasure was ruined late in 1816. In the grey dawn of 10 December, a pensioner from the Chelsea hospital saw something floating in the cold waters of the lake. When the old man got close, he realized to his horror that it was a young woman. Worse still, she was heavily pregnant.

It was quickly discovered that this was Harriet Shelley (1795–1816), the wife of the poet Percy – although her pregnancy is something of a mystery. She hadn't seen her famous husband for almost two years and the father was unknown. Adding to the confusion was the fact that Harriet herself hadn't been seen since 9 November – and that her body looked as if it had already been dead for several days.

What is clear, at least, is that Harriet was desperately unhappy. She left a suicide note for Shelley, stating:

> When you read this letr. I shall be no more an inhabitant of this miserable world. do not regret the loss of one who could never be anything but a source of vexation & misery to you all belonging to me . . . My dear Bysshe . . . if you had never

left me I might have lived but as it is, I freely forgive you &
may you enjoy that happiness which you have deprived me of
. . . so shall my spirit find rest & forgiveness. God bless you all
is the last prayer of the unfortunate Harriet S—

Shelley married Mary Wollstonecraft Godwin less than two weeks after
the body was discovered.

Trouble stalked Leigh Hunt (1784–1859), too. In 1813, the poet
and essayist was sent to Horsemonger Lane Jail in Southwark for two
years for calling the Prince Regent 'corpulent . . . a violator of his
word, a libertine' in his magazine *The Examiner*. He was at least soon
taking visits from admirers like Lord Byron, who also disliked the over-
weight royal.

Once released, Hunt moved to the Vale of Health in Hampstead
(so called – in a fine early example of capitalist double-speak – after
the once malarial swamp was drained by the Hampstead Water Company). There, he introduced Keats to Shelley in 1816. The meeting
didn't go entirely well. Keats felt patronized by Shelley's advice to publish his early poems, and bristled in the company of the more famous
and richer poet. Even so, the two men corresponded from then until
Keats's untimely death, their friendship and mutual respect deepening
over the years.

Both men had suffered, after all. Shelley might have had a wealthy
background, but his journey hadn't always been easy. As well as his
turbulent love life, he had caused a scandal when he was expelled from
Oxford for writing about atheism. Before that his time at school in
Eton had been miserable, as he was bullied for refusing to join in fag-
ging rituals and because of his disdain for sport. He had avenged himself
by trying the patience of his masters. He engaged in boxing matches
while declaiming Homer. He blew up a tree on the school grounds. He
hid a bulldog in the desk of the head teacher. He gave a tutor an electric
shock by running a current through a doorknob. He was finally sent
packing after stabbing a fellow student with a silver fork.

Keats had been born in near-poverty, the son of an ostler,

somewhere near Moorgate Station. But he at least managed to get an education – and this in spite of the death of both of his parents before he was fourteen. He had even entered himself into medical school at Guy's Hospital in 1815. (You can get a good sense of the sort of place he might have worked – and possibly actually did work – in the Old Operating Theatre there.)

Keats was still a student when he met Shelley in 1816, but was increasingly dedicating himself to literature. He was soon on something of a roll. Birdsong overheard in the garden of his small house on Wentworth Place in 1818 (now Keats Grove and the home to an excellent museum about the poet) inspired his 'Ode to a Nightingale'. According to local legend, he wrote the verses in the Spaniards Inn at Hampstead Heath while drinking a pint.

It was also in Wentworth Place that Keats fell in love: with a woman who would soon become his next-door neighbour, Fanny Brawne (1800–65). Their romance, separated by just one thin wall and tragically unconsummated, would inspire glorious letters and further poems. But a shadow fell over the young genius while he lived in that house. It was there in 1820 that he first coughed up blood and realized that he had tuberculosis. 'I know the colour of that blood; – it is arterial blood; – I cannot be deceived in that colour; – that drop of blood is my death-warrant; – I must die,' he told his room-mate Charles Brown (1787–1842).

Soon Keats was shipping out to Italy, and Shelley and Byron had also disappeared into Europe. When Keats died in Rome in 1821, Shelley wrote the poem 'Adonais' for his lost friend. When Shelley himself drowned in Spezia in 1822, he was sailing in his boat named the *Don Juan* in Byron's honour and he had a copy of Keats's poems in his pocket.

A few Romantics did stick with London for longer. The prickly critic Hazlitt stayed until his death in 1830, antagonizing conservative society with his political views, his continued sponsorship of such degenerates as Shelley and Byron, his inability to mince words and his high moral tone. 'The most insignificant people are the most

On 24 August 1806, when Mary Shelley was nine years old, Samuel Taylor Coleridge paid a visit to her father, William Godwin, at their rooms in the Polygon (near St Pancras, see p.176). Later that evening he recited 'The Rime of the Ancient Mariner' – little knowing that Mary and her sister, who had been packed off to bed, were actually hiding behind the parlour sofa. Mary never forgot the performance, and a decade later the poem would influence the opening passages of *Frankenstein*.

apt to sneer at others,' he declared. 'They are safe from reprisals. And have no hope of rising in their own self-esteem but by lowering their neighbours.' He also noted: 'When a thing ceases to be a subject of controversy, it ceases to be a subject of interest.'

He took his own advice and endeavoured to ensure that he never became boring. Possibly his greatest controversy came when he started an affair with the daughter of a Soho landlady who was half his age and wrote about it in *Liber Amoris*. This book provided just the ammunition his enemies needed to destroy his reputation, and Hazlitt died a lonely death from stomach cancer, delirious and dependent on opium in a boarding house at 6 Frith Street in Soho. His landlady at the time was so keen to let the property again that she hid his body under the bed while she showed new prospective tenants around. The site is now occupied by a hotel – Hazlitt's – and retains much of the interior that Hazlitt would have known.

Coleridge held on in London too, lasting until 1834. In 1821 he had moved in with his friend Dr James Gillman at The Grove in Highgate, intending to stay for just the few weeks it would take him to kick his laudanum habit. He ended up living there for thirteen years, and was still addicted when he died. His mental state is well conveyed in a story Hazlitt told about a visit to see the poet at The Grove. He said that while they were talking Coleridge absent-mindedly took hold of a button on his coat. When he told Coleridge he had to go, the poet didn't loosen his grip on the button ... So Hazlitt took out his penknife and cut himself free.

Leigh Hunt, finally, made it all the way to 1859, before death caught up with him in Putney. He had lived long enough to have become friends with Dickens and to witness the next great flowering of literary talent in the capital.

KEY ADDRESSES

Berry Bros & Rudd Wine Merchants, 3 St James's Street, SW1A (Tube station: Piccadilly)

Keats House, 10 Keats Grove, NW3 (Tube station: Hampstead)

The Spaniards Inn, Spaniards Road, NW3 (Tube station: Golders Green)

Old Operating Theatre, Guy's Hospital, 9a St Thomas Street, SE1 (Tube station: London Bridge)

Hazlitt's Hotel, 6 Frith Street, W1D (Tube station: Tottenham Court Road)

The Serpentine, Hyde Park (Tube station: Hyde Park Corner)

RECOMMENDED READING

Peter Ackroyd, *Chatterton*

Lord Byron, *Childe Harold's Pilgrimage*; *Don Juan*

Leigh Hunt, *The Autobiography of Leigh Hunt*

John Keats, *Collected Poems; Letters*

Percy Bysshe Shelley, *Complete Works*

CHAPTER EIGHT

EMINENT VICTORIANS AND SECRET BOHEMIANS

——————

B y 1800, London was already one of the world's biggest cities, with almost 1 million inhabitants. A century later, 6.7 million people were crowded into its fog-bound and often dangerous geography: a tangle of alleys, dark courtyards, overcrowded tenements, soot-blackened palaces, smoking factories, thronging docks and, mercifully, green, well-tended parks. The city was busier and bigger than any other place on earth – and the literary scene was correspondingly impressive. Literary titans walked those dirty, fascinating streets.

Chief among them was Charles Dickens, who would prowl for miles and miles, day and night, in search of inspiration, sometimes battling insomnia, sometimes accompanied by his pet raven 'Grip'. One night in 1857 he walked from his house in Tavistock Place in Bloomsbury to his house in Kent: thirty miles by gas-lamp and moonlight. Around this time he took so many other nocturnal promenades that he wrote an essay on the subject, 'Night Walks'. Writing in 1860 (the year that *Great Expectations* was published), he details the sights and smells of night-time London, from the ejection of the 'last brawling drunkards' into the street at pub closing time, to the huddles of fruit-sellers sharing early morning coffee at Covent Garden market. He also took in various late pie and potato sellers and dozens more who, like him, were trying to 'get through the night' when the 'wild moon and clouds were as restless as an evil conscience in a tumbled bed, and the very shadow of the immensity of London seemed to lie oppressively upon the river'.

Just about the only place that Dickens refused to walk was Old Hungerford Stairs (near the present-day site of Charing Cross Station) by the river Thames. It was near here, in 1824, that he had the awful experience of working in Warren's boot-blacking factory, aged just twelve. He had to toil ten hours a day, six days a week (for just six shillings a week), pasting labels onto pots of boot polish in 'dirty and decayed' conditions next to the stinking river. This was the lowest point in Dickens's life. His father had been imprisoned for debt in the Marshalsea (see p.107) and his family had fallen into dire poverty. Later, he would write that he felt 'utterly neglected and hopeless' and full of secret shame about his position. 'I never had the courage to go back to the place where my servitude began,' he explained to a friend. He rarely mentioned it, in fact – although the experience would colour much of his fiction. The Marshalsea appears in *Little Dorrit* when the eponymous heroine's father is sent there for debt – and it's where she spends a sizeable portion of her childhood. The blacking factory also crops up in *David Copperfield* as Murdstone and Grinby's warehouse, a filthy, scary place 'literally overrun with rats', where young David has to stick labels on wine bottles.

David Copperfield shared many other childhood experiences with Dickens – including being born outside of London. Dickens was actually born in Portsmouth in 1812, and only moved to London (at first to Norfolk Street, near St Pancras) aged three. He also spent quite a bit of his childhood in Chatham, in Kent, and eventually died in Rochester, also in Kent, in 1870 – although that is incidental. 'London' – the solitary word which made up the first sentence of his masterpiece *Bleak House* – was everything to Dickens, from first to last.

Contrary to popular belief, Dickens's first big hit wasn't *The Pickwick Papers*. After he escaped the blacking factory, he spent a few years as a pupil at Wellington House Academy in Camden Town and a year working as a clerk in a law office at Gray's Inn, and then became a reporter. His journalism formed his first published collection, largely based on a series of hugely successful articles in the *Morning Chronicle*, called *Sketches by Boz* and published in 1836. In these he declared: 'What inexhaustible food for speculation do the streets of London afford!'

That was an opinion Dickens held for the rest of his life. He called London his 'Magic Lantern' and found it hard to write if he spent too long away. His frequent method of composition was to step out into the city as he began to think of a story: 'searching for some pictures I wanted to build upon'. In the first weeks of writing *Barnaby Rudge*, for instance, he visited 'the most wretched and distressful streets' to find scenes that would inspire him to write movingly about beggars and grinding poverty – and also, again, about the excitement of walking at night.

And so it went on. Dickens spent the majority of his writing life in the English capital, and wrote mostly about its characters, its splendours and also its terror and misery. When Dickens was at his working peak, the average lifespan of London residents was twenty-seven years (twenty-two if they were working-class), and over half the funerals in London were for children under the age of ten, thanks mainly to contagious disease and malnutrition. A large percentage of six- and seven-year-olds in the city had full-time jobs. The air was thick with pollution (against which Dickens was an early campaigner) from factories and home fires. Living conditions were insanitary. Crime was rife. Dickens saw it all, and, with his tremendous talent for empathy, helped millions of other readers to share the same experiences.

He also genuinely tried to help the underclasses he wrote about – the people who made him so famous. In 1847 he set up Urania House, a sanctuary for homeless women in Shepherd's Bush, which he managed for twelve years. In those days, most homes like this were harsh and punitive, but Dickens was at pains to make sure that Urania House was run more like a welcoming home. He also campaigned tirelessly for better working conditions, better sanitation, and better treatment of children.

But mainly, Dickens wrote – incorporating everything he saw around him into those brilliant, bright, fat-to-bursting novels. The very populace of London found its way into their pages. There's some suggestion, for example, that Bill Sikes was based on a certain 'William Sykes' who sold tallow and oil for lamps in Marylebone, near Dickens's childhood house at 10 Norfolk Street. (Nine doors down from the Norfolk Street rooms was a workhouse that would later form the basis of the one in *Oliver Twist*.) Dickens didn't have to go far for Micawber, either – the man, in fact, followed him from house to house in London, because it was his own father. Fagin was based on the real-life Londoner Isaac 'Ikey' Solomon, who fenced stolen goods from a jewellery store near Petticoat Lane. Ebenezer Scrooge was inspired by the notoriously miserly MP John Elwes (1714–89) – better known as 'Elwes the Miser' – and this despite inheriting a large fortune from his uncle (something like £18 million in today's money). Rather than enjoy the high life, Elwes went to bed as soon as the sun set, in order to save candles; he wore his clothes until they fell apart; and he let his house fall into disrepair, rather than pay for its upkeep. Magistrate Fang, the unjust judge in *Oliver Twist*, was a direct and deliberate copy of Allan Stewart Laing (1788–1862) – a notoriously corrupt justice who was dismissed from the bench in 1838, and whom Dickens specifically said he would be lampooning in his 'next issue of *Oliver*'. Another of Dickens's London neighbours, Jane Seymour Hill, a manicurist and chiropodist, saw herself modelled in Miss Mowcher – and threatened legal action. Dickens mollified her with some well-timed heroism on the part of the character.

Yet while people were important, Dickens remarked that it was the city of London itself that formed the greatest and most important character of them all. There is hardly a borough or quarter that doesn't appear in a Dickens novel. Walk through Covent Garden, and you'll be within a stone's throw of the flower market where David Copperfield bought flowers for Dora, or the theatre where he attends a showing of *Julius Caesar*. Stroll on to Holborn and you'll find 58 Lincoln's Inn Fields, the house of Dickens's friend (and future biographer) John Forster (1812–76) and the inspiration for Mr Tulkington's house in *Bleak House*. Go a little north and you're in Clerkenwell and Saffron Hill, described in the time of Dickens as a 'squalid neighbourhood, a home of dodgers and thieves' – and the location of Fagin's Den. Clerkenwell Green was the scene of Oliver's risible attempt at pick-pocketing. Nearby, Bleeding Heart Yard was the location for Doyce and Clennam's factory in *Little Dorrit*. You're also near 'The City' – the financial centre of London and the medieval city, where Scrooge (*A Christmas Carol*) has his offices, alongside Paul Dombey in *Dombey and Son* (in Leadenhall Street), Anthony Chuzzlewit (*Martin Chuzzlewit*) and Fascination Fledgeby (*Our Mutual Friend*). Cornhill is where Bob Cratchit slides down the ice on his way home. Head east to Bethnal Green, where poor Nancy, found out by Fagin and Bill Sikes, is murdered in a slum house. Go west to Mayfair and Cavendish Square, where in *Nicholas Nickleby* Madame Mantalini has her dressmaking shop; and the Albany, where – when he isn't working in the City – Fascination Fledgeby lives in a bachelor flat. Cross the river to Southwark – haunted by Little Dorrit, who was christened and married in the church of St George the Martyr, and like Dickens's poor old dad, lived in the Marshalsea Debtors' Prison. The stories stretch as far east from there as Greenwich and the Trafalgar Tavern – one of Dickens's own favourite pubs, which appears in *Our Mutual Friend* as the setting for a wedding breakfast. (In the same novel, Bella and John Rokesmith marry in the church at Greenwich.) Go west again and you'll hit Richmond and Eel Pie Island, where Miss Kenning attends a party in *Nicholas Nickleby*.

Dickens himself, meanwhile, occupied addresses all over the city. Set aside a good day if you want to pay homage to all of them:

1815–17:	10 Norfolk Street (now 22 Cleveland Street), St Pancras
1822–4:	16 Bayham Street, Camden (the model for the Cratchits' home in *A Christmas Carol*)
1824:	4 Gower Street North, Fitzrovia
1824:	Little College Street, Camden
1824–7:	29 Johnson Street, Somers Town
1827–9:	The Polygon, Somers Town
1829–32:	10 Norfolk Street, Fitzroy Square, Fitzrovia

1832:	15 Fitzroy Street, Fitzrovia
1833:	18 Bentinck Street, Marylebone
1834:	Cecil Street, Covent Garden
1834:	Buckingham Street, Covent Garden
1834–5:	13 Furnival's Inn, Holborn
1835:	11 Selwood Terrace, Brompton
1836:	16 Furnival's Inn, Holborn
1837–8:	48 Doughty Street, Holborn
1838–9:	A cottage somewhere in Twickenham
1839–51:	1 Devonshire Terrace, Bayswater
1848:	3 Chester Place, Regent's Park
1851–60:	Tavistock House, Bloomsbury
1870:	5 Hyde Park Place, Mayfair

In Doughty Street there is now a museum dedicated to Dickens, with a collection of manuscripts, paintings and Dickens's own furniture. Opposite the house, there's another blue plaque: 'Sydney Smith 1771–1843 Author and wit lived here'. It's piquant to imagine how Smith must have felt as he looked out across the road, knowing that his neighbour was so easily eclipsing him. It was at Doughty Street that 'The Inimitable' finished the *Pickwick Papers* and wrote *Oliver Twist*, *Nicholas Nickleby* and the opening of *Barnaby Rudge*. There too he held numerous dinner parties for increasingly famous friends like Leigh Hunt and John Forster. Smith, in contrast, is probably most famous now for asking, 'Who reads an American book?' – a question posterity has answered resoundingly.

Smith was also a clergyman and declared his own sermons to be 'long and vigorous – like the penis of a jackass'. History, alas, has not recorded much about Dickens's own member, but it is notable that while he lived in Doughty Street he also married his first wife Catherine – and fell in love with her sister Mary. Mary died tragically, aged just seventeen, and became the model for Rose Maylie in *Oliver Twist* and Little Nell in *The Old Curiosity Shop*.

Dickens's marriage continued to be unconventional. Another sister

A DICKENSIAN PUB CRAWL

Start out at the **George Inn** (77 Borough High Street, SE1). This is the very last of London's galleried coaching inns – where Dickens drank himself. He also mentioned the pub in *Little Dorrit*, and his – Dickens's – life insurance policy hangs on the wall.

Take a fifteen-minute stroll across London Bridge and up to Leadenhall Market, where at 3 Castle Court you'll find the **George and Vulture**, the London base of Pickwick and his friends, which is mentioned more than twenty times in the novel. Pickwick has a particular liking for their port (served, in those days, by the pint).

A further twenty-minute walk along Cheapside will take you to **Ye Olde Cheshire Cheese**. Dickens first started drinking at this pub when he was a young reporter on Fleet Street, and it remained one of his favourites in the city. Apparently, he liked to sit at the table to the right of the fireplace in the ground-floor room, opposite the bar. (It's where Sydney Carton takes Charles Darnay for 'a good plain dinner and plain wine' in *A Tale of Two Cities*.)

Then cut through Shoe Lane and through to Saffron Hill and the **One Tun** – another regular haunt of Dickens and quite possibly the basis for the Three Cripples pub in *Oliver Twist* (the favoured drinking spot of Bill Sikes and his gang of thieves). Fagin lived nearby.

Next, head towards Holborn at the **Cittie Of Yorke**. This used to be the Grey's Inn Coffee House, where David Copperfield stops to ask after his friend Tommy Traddles. The rioters in *Barnaby Rudge* also hide in the cellars.

Cut through Lincoln's Inn Fields and past the **Old Curiosity Shop** to the **George IV**, renamed the Magpie and Stump in *The Pickwick Papers* and known (in that novel) for the 500,000 barrels of stout it kept in its cellars.

A further ten minutes' stroll, down Russell Street and into Covent Garden, will bring you to the **Lamb and Flag**, which boasts a little plaque in the alleyway, commemorating Dickens's time spent propping up the bar. In his days, the tavern had a slightly more alarming name: *The Bucket of Blood*.

Finally, head across Shaftesbury Avenue and into Soho's Greek Street, where the **Pillars of Hercules** was almost certainly the Hercules Pillars in *A Tale of Two Cities*. (It's kept its literary credentials here: Ian McEwan, Julian Barnes and Martin Amis were all regulars, and Clive James named his second book of literary criticism after it: *At the Pillars of Hercules*.)

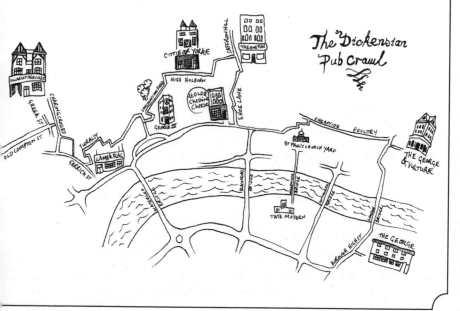

of Catherine's, Georgina, also lived with the writer from 1842 until his death. But Catherine herself moved out in 1858 after Charles fell in love with the eighteen-year-old actress Ellen Ternan. This was not the way respectable Victorians were expected to do things – and the affair was hushed up until long after Dickens's death.

Plenty of other writers had secrets of their own. Behind closed doors, few of the stars of literary London in the nineteenth century conformed to the staid and starched stereotypes we often entertain about them today. In their own way, they were often more forward-thinking and more revolutionary than the brigades of modernists, Fitzrovians and Bloomsberries who came after them (and who derided them for being such stick-in-the-muds).

Dickens's long-time friend and occasional rival Wilkie Collins (1824–89), for one, was an avowed bohemian. He objected to marriage as an institution, but fell deeply in love with a woman called Caroline Graves (c.1830–95) in 1858. She was a humble shopkeeper who lived around the corner from his apartment on Howland Street; the two moved in together and cohabited (to the horror of his respectable and religious mother) until his death in 1889 – though from 1868 he also kept house with Martha Rudd (1845–1919), who he met on a seaside research trip to Winterton in Norfolk. Collins and Rudd had three children together.

Caroline Graves was further notable as inspiration for Dickens's Miss Havisham, not to mention Collins's 'Woman in White'. Collins liked to tell people that he met Graves while on a night-time walk with his brother Charles (1828–73) and the pre-Raphaelite painter John Everett Millais (1829–96). According to Collins, during this stroll they had come across a beautiful and distraught woman, and learned, upon questioning her, that she had escaped from a flat in Regent's Park where a man with strange, mesmeric abilities had been keeping her prisoner. This was entirely untrue – but it didn't stop Millais's son corroborating and expanding on the story in his later biography of his father.

The Woman in White was first serialized in Charles Dickens's magazine *All the Year Round*, between 1859 and 1860, and a craze swept through London when it first came out. It was the most popular serial that the journal ever ran – and when it was first published in one volume in 1860, in a limited run of 1,000, it sold out in less than a day. By this time it was also possible to buy Woman in White cloaks and bonnets, Woman in White perfume, and sheet music inspired by the book. In the previous year, while the serialization was still running its course and people did not yet know the outcome of the story, bets were taken about what the awful 'secret' at the heart of the book might be, and men wrote to Collins asking for the real-life identity of the novel's heroine Marian Halcombe, so that they could ask for her hand in marriage.

It was the novel for the time – a rich mix of sensation and scandal, inspired, as well as by Caroline Graves, by current goings-on in London. There was a new wave of 'penny journalism' on Fleet Street, a genre fascinated by sexual gossip, poisonings and the criminal underworld (particularly where it mixed with, or 'impersonated', high society). There was also an unfolding scandal involving one of Dickens's associates, London society-goer and occasional poet Lord Lytton (1803–73), who had fallen out with his wife and had her locked up in an asylum. Finally, in the years that *The Woman in White* was serialized, London was 'crawling' (as Collins put it) with Neapolitan and French spies – something that the public thrilled to (stories of them using the Great Exhibition as a pretext for coming over were especially popular) – and Collins made good use of their presence in his characterization of Count Fosco. And although large parts of the novel itself take place outside of the city, it also starts – crucially – in Hartright's mother's cosy cottage in Hampstead, and with the wandering of the eponymous woman in white on Hampstead Heath.

The book made Collins's fortune – and set the course for a wonderful decade, culminating in the publication of *The Moonstone* in 1868. Sadly, after this the writer's fortunes faded. He became a habitual user of opium – through necessity as much as choice, since he originally began to take it to counter the painful symptoms of gout. Collins also fell out with his great friend Dickens. For years, the pair had often been seen walking together in Covent Garden and the Strand, but this ebbed away after Wilkie's brother Charles married Dickens's daughter Kate in 1860. Dickens wasn't keen on Charles Collins, whom he found 'sickly' and 'weak', and the novelist's treatment of him affected the two friends' relationship. The extent of the rift is reflected in Collins's more private feelings about his colleague's work, which were found after his death, in the library he had accumulated at his house in Wimpole Street. He wrote of *Dombey and Son* as a book that: 'no intelligent person can have read without astonishment at the badness of it'. He described the unfinished *Edwin Drood* as 'the melancholy work of a worn out brain'. And on the first page of John Forster's biography, where the adoring author declares 'Charles Dickens, the most popular novelist of the century', Collins added: '. . . *after Walter Scott*'.

Despite all of this, Wilkie was devastated when Charles Dickens died. Of their early years of friendship, he wrote, 'We saw each other every day, and were as fond of each other as men could be.'

Collins himself died aged sixty-five in 1889 in Taunton Place, having lived his whole life in London. He is remembered with approval now, but at least one fellow Victorian literary Londoner didn't think much of his writing. Anthony Trollope (1815–82) wrote in his autobiography of Collins's style: 'The construction is most minute and most wonderful. But I can never lose the taste of the construction.'

Trollope was born in London and went to Harrow School – although he also spent time in Bruges, among other places, where the family ended up after fleeing from debtors. In 1834 Trollope returned to London, where he took up a job with the General Post Office. At first he didn't shine, acquiring a reputation for unpunctuality and insubordination. Matters weren't helped by the fact that Trollope took after his father in the care of his finances – and a moneylender daily visited him at his workplace, demanding the repayment of £200. But he made up for it in 1852, designing the modern, free-standing red post box whose successors can still be seen all over London.

As an adult, Trollope lived in Ireland for some years and travelled widely – but he did take considerable inspiration from his home town. His 1875 masterpiece, one of the last great serialized Victorian novels, *The Way We Live Now*, centres on a corrupt city financier called Augustus Melmotte. In it, Trollope wastes no time in laying into London, portraying it as a luxurious, decayed centre of limitless credit and debased relationships:

> If dishonesty can live in a gorgeous palace with pictures on all its walls, and gems in all its cupboards, with marble and ivory in all its corners, and can give Apician dinners, and get into Parliament, and deal in millions, then dishonesty is not disgraceful, and the man dishonest after such a fashion is not a low scoundrel.

In *The Way We Live Now*, both the Liberals and the Conservatives vie to put Melmotte forward as their parliamentary candidate – and no one could care less whether he's a fraudster or not, as long as he looks the part and pleases the masses. It could almost be about – well, the way we live now.

Also courted by Liberals and Conservatives – and possibly even less suited to the life of a politician than Augustus Melmotte – was Alfred, Lord Tennyson. Both the Liberal Prime Minister Gladstone (1809–98) and the Tory Prime Minister (and novelist) Benjamin Disraeli (1804–81) spent years trying to persuade the poet to take a lordship. He finally accepted it in 1884, when urged to do so by Queen Victoria, in spite of grave reservations and his unconventional (for the time) dislike of Christianity and its associated rituals.

Tennyson, who was born in Lincolnshire, spent much of his long life in London and wrote about it many times. Although he was happy to be wooed by high society, and served as poet laureate during the height of the British Empire, some of his London poetry also shows curious ambivalence about Britain's role in the world. As well as his indictment of the blunder that led to the ill-fated charge of the Light Brigade, he also raised a few objections when the obelisk now known as Cleopatra's Needle was carried from Egypt to be placed on the Victoria Embankment. The Dean of Westminster Cathedral and Egyptologist

Arthur Stanley (1815–81) asked him to write a poem to be carved into the base of the monument. Tennyson wrote a poem – but he also told Londoners, speaking in the voice of the obelisk:

> . . . *your own citizens, for their own renown,*
> *Through strange seas drew me to your monster town.*
> *I have seen the four great empires disappear.*
> *I was when London was not. I am here.*

Elsewhere, Tennyson could be even more grumpy about his adopted city. He wrote one poem cursing an East End pub: 'Black Bull of Aldgate, may thy horns rot from the sockets!' (Posterity has granted his wish; the pub has long since been demolished.) But his greatest moment came in less amusing circumstances. *In Memoriam*, published in 1850, was written about the poet's grief at the death of his friend Arthur Hallam (1811–33). Hallam had lived at 67 Wimpole Street, just to the north-west of Oxford Circus, and part of the poem recounts how Tennyson, after Hallam's death, would haunt the street outside his friend's London home:

> *Dark house, by which once more I stand*
>   *Here in the long unlovely street,*
>   *Doors, where my heart was used to beat*
> *So quickly, waiting for a hand,*
>
> *A hand that can be clasp'd no more –*
>   *Behold me, for I cannot sleep,*
>   *And like a guilty thing I creep*
> *At earliest morning to the door.*
>
> *He is not here; but far away*
>   *The noise of life begins again,*
>   *And ghastly thro' the drizzling rain*
> *On the bald street breaks the blank day.*

While Tennyson was grieving, a rather happier affair was taking place a few doors down at 50 Wimpole Street. This was the house of the poet Elizabeth Barrett (1806–81). During 1845, her fellow versifier Robert Browning (1812–89) became a regular visitor, after falling hard for her 1844 volume *Poems*. 'I love your verses with all my heart, dear Miss Barrett,' Browning wrote to her, extolling their 'affluent language' and 'fresh strange music'.

Soon the two were making a different kind of music together, meeting in secret because they knew Barrett's overbearing father would not approve, and arranging a hush-hush marriage in St Marylebone Parish Church in the late summer of 1846.

The following year, London witnessed another secret marriage – this one fictional, when Captain Rawdon Crawley sneaked off to marry Becky Sharp in William Makepeace Thackeray's *Vanity Fair*.

Thackeray wrote his great satire of London high society while living at 13 (now 16) Young Street, Kensington (he wrote the mighty *Pendennis* and *History of Henry Esmond* in the same house, which he occupied between 1846 and 1853). Years later, when he was walking past the building with a friend, he shouted, 'Down on your knees, you rogue, for here *Vanity Fair* was penned, and I will go down with you, for I have a high opinion of that little production myself.'

His daughter Minnie wasn't quite so keen on the novel. As Thackeray related in a letter, she once looked up from breakfast and said, 'Papa, why do you not write books like *Nicholas Nickleby*?' Charles Dickens was just as dubious about *Vanity Fair* – but mainly because it was so well received and selling 7,000 copies a week. Thackeray used some of the profits from the novel to build a swish house at 2 Palace Green (which these days houses the Israeli embassy).

Before he left Young Street, however, he had a fateful meeting with Charlotte Brontë (1816–55). Brontë had dedicated *Jane Eyre* to him, not realizing that this was a terrible mistake because, like Rochester in her novel, Thackeray had a little-known wife whom he had hidden away. Similar misunderstandings abounded when he organized a party in Charlotte's honour during one of her visits to London in 1849.

The trouble this time was that she refused to acknowledge that she was 'Currer Bell', even though it was well known by then that she was the woman behind the pseudonym on the cover of *Jane Eyre*. She also gave only sharp, short answers when questioned. 'I do and I don't,' she said simply when other guests asked if she liked London society women. The atmosphere grew so strained that Thackeray sneaked out of his own party to go to his club. Anne, another of Thackeray's caustic daughters, later recalled:

> This then is the authoress, the unknown power whose books have set all London talking, reading, speculating . . . We all smile as my father stoops to offer his arm; for, genius as she may be, Miss Brontë can barely reach his elbow . . . And everyone waited for the brilliant conversation which never began at all.

William, the gentlemanly author, still visited Charlotte the next day, and when she got back to her home in Haworth she wrote an excited letter to her friend Ellen Nussey: 'I feel as if I had come out of an exciting whirl.'

As to why everyone knew that Charlotte was Currer Bell: this was down to Charlotte herself, who had recently presented herself to her own publisher. On 8 July 1848, she and her sister Anne (1820–49) decided that they were going to travel down from Yorkshire to London and call on Messrs Smith and Elder, thus clearing up the confusion over the authorship of their novels. Travelling through the night and arriving the next day at Paternoster Row, they stepped from their coach with some misgivings at their impetuousness – but made their way the half-mile or so to Cornhill nonetheless, announcing themselves with some agitation. For his part, the publisher John Smith was amazed that the author of *Jane Eyre* (which owed some of its popularity to being an 'improper' book) was a diminutive, startled-looking woman. As for the Brontës, they may have been somewhat surprised that their publisher, quite unlike the elderly man with whiskers they imagined, was actually a handsome boy of twenty-three.

Charlotte was also possibly relieved to have survived a visit to London at all. In her early years, she thought it a place of unimaginable sin. When her friend Ellen Nussey visited the city in 1834, Charlotte even wrote a letter to her afterwards, expressing her astonishment that Ellen had returned 'unchanged'.

'It is a very remarkable book: we have no remembrance of another combining such genuine power with such horrid taste.'
Elizabeth Rigby reviews *Jane Eyre* in the *Quarterly Review*

If Thackeray's dinner party had been awkward, it had nothing on the party thrown to celebrate the publication of George Eliot's *Silas Marner* held at Greenwich Observatory in 1861. Eliot (1819–80) was the only female present, as no other ladies could dine with a 'fallen woman'.

Eliot was treated with appalling rudeness by polite female society because she was at that point living 'in sin' at 31 Wimbledon Park Road with George Henry Lewes (1817–78), Goethe's biographer.

The writer came from Nuneaton, but had moved to London aged thirty-one, in 1850 – much to the consternation of her family. She stayed first at 142 the Strand, the office, bookshop and home of the radical publisher John Chapman (1821–94). There, according to some scholars, she had a brief affair with Chapman himself (despite the presence of his wife, children and live-in mistress), and also started editing *The Westminster Review*, a progressive journal that Chapman had recently acquired. In its pages she published Leigh Hunt and Thackeray, and vocally pressed for suffrage. She worked tirelessly for five years before running off with one of the journal's contributors.

In spite of her popularity and her glittering career, when George Eliot died in 1880 she wasn't buried in Westminster Abbey – being deemed unacceptable, thanks to her 'denial of the Christian faith' and 'untoward' relationship with George Henry Lewes. She's buried instead next to her lover in Highgate, in the area traditionally reserved for religious dissenters and agnostics. But at least Eliot took her pleasures. Indeed, throughout her life she had a number of other liaisons, and seems to have caught the eye of several of the leading radical intellectuals of the time. The pre-Raphaelite William Rossetti (1829–1919) told everyone that he had seen Herbert Spencer (1820–1903), philosopher, political theorist and originator of the phrase 'survival of the fittest', who was first published by John Chapman, proposing to her on the steps of Somerset House.

The Rossetti family, in turn, were equally dedicated to the road less travelled. William's brother Dante Gabriel (1828–81) lived near George Eliot at 16 Cheyne Walk in Chelsea, in a house full of wolves, jackdaws, lizards and peacocks. (The latter so annoyed the neighbours that they've been banned from the street ever since.) George Meredith (1828–1909) lived in the same house for a year in 1862, as did Algernon Swinburne (1837–1909) – before he decamped to 3 Great James Street. (The critic and novelist Theodore Watts-Dunton (1832–1914) visited this latter address to find the poet 'stark naked with his aureole of red hair flying around his head performing a Dionysiac dance'. Swinburne chased him out.)

Also in 1862, Dante Gabriel's wife Elizabeth Siddal (born 1829) died tragically young from a laudanum overdose. Dante buried her in Highgate Cemetery, alongside his most recent, unpublished, collection of poems. These remained with her until 1869, when her late husband, having fallen on hard times, obtained permission to dig up the grave and retrieve them. The poems made him so much money that he was able to stay in Chelsea and continue as before.

Dante's sister Christina (1830–94), another leading pre-Raphaelite, benefited from Highgate associations too, since her famous poem *Goblin Market* was inspired by her volunteer work at the St Mary Magdalene 'house of charity' in Highgate, a refuge for prostitutes where she helped out from 1859 to 1870.

Graveyards also figured strongly in the career of Thomas Hardy. In the mid-1860s Hardy took a job with an architect's firm. One of his jobs was to survey the St Pancras graveyard, where the new Midland train line was about to run. Specifically, he had to supervise the removal of corpses. One, he said, had two heads. He relocated dozens of gravestones to a corner of the graveyard where they stand still, with an ash tree – known as the Hardy tree – thrusting up from among them. He wrote a novel based on the experience (which was rejected – the decision at the publisher's made by the poet George Meredith). Hardy recalled the experience in a poem too, called 'The Levelled Churchyard':

O passenger, pray list and catch
Our sighs and piteous groans,
Half stifled in this jumbled patch
Of wrenched memorial stones!

We late-lamented, resting here,
Are mixed to human jam,
And each to each exclaims in fear,
'I know not which I am!'

As these lines suggest, Hardy didn't think much of his job. In fact, it made him ill. He quit, and retreated to the countryside – which is probably why, in 1923 (years after his death in 1900), the spirit of Oscar Wilde (born 1854) told the London spiritualist Hester Dowden that Hardy was a 'harmless rustic'. According to Mrs Dowden, the deceased wit described *Ulysses* as 'a great bulk of filth' and declared: 'Being dead is the most boring experience in life. That is, if one excepts being married or dining with a schoolmaster.' Arthur Conan Doyle pronounced these messages 'the most final evidence of a continued personality that we have'.

Absurd as all that may be, Dowden still released a book of her conversations with the late dandy in the 1920s. The memoir caused a large stir in the city, too, showing just how much fascination Wilde continued to exert after the close of the Victorian era – and after his career was brought to its dismal end, in poverty and exile, in Paris.

Wilde's death was in stark contrast to his first arrival in London, flying high in 1878 after graduating with one of the best firsts in Greats that Oxford University had ever seen ('the dons,' he wrote gleefully, 'were astonished'). He'd quickly set himself up with his father's inheritance (the last of it) as a bachelor about town, taking lodgings at 1 (now 44) Tite Street, Chelsea. From this base, he set about dazzling London society. By the end of May 1884 he had written a play, published a poetry collection and married Constance Lloyd at the Anglican St James' Parish Church in Paddington – the latter of which brought in another handy £250 a year (from Constance's father) and also allowed him to move up the road, to 16 Tite Street, and decorate it lavishly.

> **'Oh, I love London Society! It has immensely improved. It is entirely composed now of beautiful idiots and brilliant lunatics. Just what Society should be . . .'**
>
> Oscar Wilde

It wasn't long before Wilde put his flair for socializing to good use in journalism: he became a chatty, fluent contributor to the *Pall Mall Gazette* and other London magazines, taking in everything from fashion to child-rearing, politics and the arts. These were good times. Gilbert and Sullivan mentioned him in a play and his wit lit up the London salons and restaurants (among his favourites was the Café Royal, where Wilde had lunch each day at 1 p.m.; you can still drink in the same surroundings – in the appropriately renamed Oscar Wilde Bar).

> **'Thirty-five is a very attractive age. London society is full of women of the very highest birth who have, of their own free choice, remained thirty-five for years.'**
>
> Oscar Wilde

Wilde's fame grew further when the magazine editor Joseph Stoddart persuaded him to write a novel – *The Picture of Dorian Gray* – at a supper party at the Langham Hotel in 1889. (At the same party he also persuaded Conan Doyle to write *The Sign of Four*; Doyle, who was

Another of Oscar Wilde's favoured London restaurants was Kettner's on Romilly Street in Soho – where he once, scandalously, kissed a waiter. It's still open and if you do get the chance to visit, you'll be keeping good company. In the late nineteenth century Edward VII used it as a meeting place with his mistress, Lillie Langtry. Langtry was an actress, and in order to avoid gossip a secret tunnel was built between Kettner's and the nearby Palace Theatre, where she performed.

as taken with Wilde in life as in death, based a character – Thaddeus Sholto – upon him.) *Dorian Gray* was first published in *Lippincott's* magazine in 1890. Reviewers condemned it as immoral, mawkish and hedonistic, and W. H. Smith was so scandalized that it withdrew every single issue of *Lippincott's* from its railway station bookstalls. Naturally, the story (and *Lippincott's*) became all the more popular as a result – although Wilde was pressurized into toning down sexual references in later editions.

Wilde next set about conquering the London stage, with hit plays like *Salome*, *Lady Windermere's Fan*, *A Woman of No Importance*, *An Ideal Husband*, and in 1895 the immortal *The Importance of Being Earnest*. Yet even as his public life was reaching a glittering pinnacle, his personal life was about to reach a nadir.

'**Mr Wilde has brains, and art, and style, but if he can write for none but outlawed noblemen and perverted telegraph boys, the sooner he takes to tailoring (or some other decent trade) the better for his own reputation and the public morals.**'

The Scots Observer

Wilde was gay. At some point in London he was introduced to the seventeen-year-old Robert Ross (1869–1918), later an art critic, dealer, and Wilde's executor, who became his first male lover in 1886. He had other male lovers, and successfully kept them secret from the prurient general public, until one day in June 1894 he received a visit from the Marquess of Queensberry (1844–1900) at his address in Tite Street. 'I do not say that you are it,' declared the pugilistic aristocrat, 'but you look it, and pose at it, which is just as bad. And if I catch you and my son again in any public restaurant I will thrash you.'

> **'The man who can dominate a London dinner-table can dominate the world.'**
>
> Oscar Wilde

Queensberry was furious that Wilde was seeing his son Lord Alfred Douglas (1870–1945), and although he didn't thrash Wilde, he did destroy him. After six months more of public arguments in restaurants and clubs about the city, the climax came on 18 February 1895, four nights after the triumphant opening night of *The Importance of Being Earnest* at St James's Theatre, when Queensberry left a card at Wilde's club, The Albemarle, inscribed: 'For Oscar Wilde, posing somdomite [*sic*]'.

Against the advice of his friends, Wilde brought a criminal libel charge against Queensberry, but the Marquess employed detectives to prove that he was telling the truth and that Wilde did indeed see men. It was Wilde who ended up going to jail. One of his last sights of London was of the station at Clapham Junction, where he was made to stand on the platform in prison clothes, waiting for a connecting train to Reading. A member of the public came up and spat on him. That was in May 1895. He was released in May 1897, after two years' hard labour. Upon his release, he sailed immediately for France – and died soon after, on 30 November 1900, a martyr to his times. Queen Victoria herself died less than two months later. It was the end of an era. Give or take the odd ghost.

KEY ADDRESSES

Café Royal Hotel, 68 Regent Street, W1B (Tube station: Piccadilly)

Kettner's Restaurant, 29 Romilly Street, W1D (Tube station: Covent Garden)

Charles Dickens Museum, 48 Doughty Street, WC1N (Tube station: Russell Square)

Thackeray's house, 16 Young Street, W8 (Tube station: High Street Kensington)

The Hardy Tree, St Pancras Old Church, NW1 (Tube station: St Pancras)

RECOMMENDED READING

Charlotte Brontë, *Jane Eyre*

Wilkie Collins, *The Woman in White*

Charles Dickens, *Bleak House*

William Thackeray, *Vanity Fair*

Anthony Trollope, *The Way We Live Now*

Oscar Wilde, *The Picture of Dorian Gray*

CHAPTER NINE
CRIME . . .

The first great detective novel was written in London.[1] This was *The Moonstone*, written in 1868 by Wilkie Collins, and it introduced many elements which would become linchpins of the genre: a country house robbery, red herrings, false suspects, a reconstruction of the crime, a gentleman detective (Franklin Blake) and a policeman companion, Sergeant Cuff, based on the real-life Inspector Jonathan Whicher (1814–81) of Scotland Yard.

As well as playing a crucial role in *The Moonstone*, Jonathan Whicher also inspired Mr Bucket in Charles Dickens's *Bleak House*. More recently, he became the subject of *The Suspicions of Mr Whicher* by Kate Summerscale (1965–).

The Moonstone is memorable for more than its innovations. It is a fine book in its own right, with superb comedy and mystery and vivid depictions of danger and opium addiction. G. K. Chesterton (1874–1936) called it 'probably the best detective tale in the world' and Dorothy L. Sayers (1893–1957) said it was 'the finest detective story ever written'.

Chesterton and Sayers were writing more than a generation after *The Moonstone* was published in 1868, during what became known as the Golden Age of Detective Fiction, roughly stretching from the end of the nineteenth century until the Second World War. London, as so

1 As opposed to the first great detective story, which was written by Edgar Allen Poe and set – alas – in Paris.

often, dominated. But *The Moonstone* wasn't the only big influence on the Golden Age. Its writers all also followed the trail laid by that great Victorian crime solver Sherlock Holmes.

Sherlock Holmes, like Wilkie Collins's detective, was modelled on a real-life character – this time Joseph Bell (1837–1911), the man who had taught Arthur Conan Doyle when he was training to become a doctor in Edinburgh. It was from Bell that Doyle took some of Holmes's eccentric lifestyle, along with a deductive scientific approach to everything – especially crime.

Sherlock Holmes first appeared in print in 1887, in *A Study in Scarlet*. This was sold to the London publisher Ward Lock and Co for the princely sum of £25 (in full: no royalties). No one else had wanted to take it on. More fool them. Holmes quickly became a phenomenon, and so famous that there must now be few literate adults in the English-speaking world who don't know that Holmes lived at 221b Baker Street. Even if not all of them know that this address was fictional.

No matter. Plenty of the city that Holmes stalked was real enough. 'It is a hobby of mine to have an exact knowledge of London,' the sleuth once said – thus, incidentally, inventing the concept of 'The Knowledge' and the mastery of the streets and byways that London's black cab drivers are still expected to attain today.

I n a glorious case of life cashing in on art, there is now a 221b Baker Street, home of the Sherlock Holmes Museum. Confusingly, you'll find it between street numbers 237 and 241.

The London that Holmes knew was cobblestoned, fog-bound and full of dark alleyways and nasty surprises. In 'The Adventure of the Illustrious Client', in 1902, for instance, Sherlock Holmes is attacked on Regent Street and 'beaten about the head and body' by two men with sticks, 'receiving injuries' which doctors describe 'as most serious'. In 'The Final Problem', off Oxford Street and at the junction of Bentinck

Street and Welbeck Street, Sherlock is nearly killed by a runaway van.

Small wonder that Watson calls London 'a giant cesspool'. On its thoroughfares, he saw more than his fair share of dead bodies, murderers, blackmailers and thieves. There was, however, a plus side. In the Holmes novels, London's hotels are always full of intrigue (like the Langham Hotel, where the King of Bohemia stays in – yes – *The Scandal of Bohemia*), its shops offer delights (like the Stradivarius violin Holmes picks up on Tottenham Court Road), and there's always the dark wooden sanctuary of Simpson's-in-the-Strand, where Holmes and Watson like to retreat for 'something nutritious'. If you're feeling flush, you can do the same. Simpson's still sells decidedly old-fashioned English meals and looks much as Conan Doyle would have known it. Alas, the same can't be said for the Criterion, over the road, which was where Watson popped in for a drink just before his very first introduction to Holmes. The restaurant continued to function – and with the same plush gold surroundings – into the twenty-first century, but has recently been a casualty of spiralling rents (a crime in itself). Nor will you be able to go to the Diogenes Club, the gentlemen's club on Pall Mall co-founded by Sherlock Holmes's brother Mycroft, where no talking is allowed. The Diogenes Club is fictional – although Conan Doyle was himself a member of three real-life London clubs: the Reform, the Athenaeum and the Royal Automobile Club, whose atmosphere permeates his novels.

'It is my belief, Watson, founded upon my experience, that the lowest and vilest alleys in London do not present a more dreadful record of sin than does the smiling and beautiful countryside.'

Sherlock Holmes, in
The Adventure of the Copper Beeches

Conan Doyle, for his part, was among that rare breed that didn't actually delight in Sherlock Holmes's eccentricities and adventures. He once wrote to his mother from his doctor's practice in Marylebone's Wimpole Street (where he also wrote his first five novels), declaring ambivalence towards his creation. 'I think of slaying Holmes,' he said, 'and winding him up for good and all. He takes my mind from better things.' To which his mother replied, 'You won't! You can't! You mustn't!' He didn't. Not permanently, anyway. And so Holmes went on having adventures until deep into the 1920s.

By this time the Golden Age was in full swing, and there were plenty more sleuths righting wrongs around London. One of the most popular was G. K. Chesterton's Father Brown, who was, in many ways, the anti-Holmes. Holmes delights in logical deduction and suffers from a chronic empathy deficit. Father Brown's successes rely more on intuition, on imagining – empathizing with – the murderer. He once said, 'You see, I had murdered them all myself . . . I had planned out each of the crimes very carefully. I had thought out exactly how a thing like that could be done, and in what style or state of mind a man could really do it. And when I was quite sure that I felt exactly like the murderer myself, of course I knew who he was.'

The first Father Brown story, 'The Blue Cross', was published in 1910 in *The Saturday Post*. It involves Father Brown leaving a trail of clues for the Parisian detective Valentin around the city, from the West End to Hampstead Heath. The rest of the first two volumes of short stories are also set entirely in London. Few exact locations are mentioned, but throughout the stories Father Brown roams from Soho to Victoria, Hampstead Heath to Wimbledon Common, Piccadilly to the northern suburbs, trailing murderous policemen and victims dispatched by means as diverse as deathly boomerangs and hammers dropped from church spires. He also sometimes catches that recent invention the London bus, noting on one occasion: 'It was one of those journeys on which a man perpetually feels that now at last he must have come to the end of the universe, and then finds that he has only come to the beginning of Tufnell Park.'

The London Detection Club was a society set up in 1930 by a group of mystery writers including Agatha Christie, Dorothy L. Sayers and G. K. Chesterton. The group exchanged letters, met for dinner and helped each other with the nuts and bolts of their writing. Members had to agree to a code of ethics – including, in their novels and stories, pledging to give the reader a fair chance at guessing the guilty party – and also enjoyed an eccentric initiation ceremony, involving the following oath:

Q: Do you promise that your detectives shall well and truly detect the crimes presented to them using those wits which it may please you to bestow upon them and not placing reliance on nor making use of Divine Revelation, Feminine Intuition, Mumbo Jumbo, Jiggery-Pokery, Coincidence, or Act of God?

A: I do.

Q: Do you solemnly swear never to hide a vital clue from the reader?

A: I do.

Q: Do you promise to observe a seemly moderation in the use of Gangs, Conspiracies, Death-rays, Ghosts, Hypnotism, Trap-doors, Chinamen, Super-criminals and Lunatics; and utterly and forever to forswear Mysterious Potions unknown to Science?

A: I do.

Q: Will you honour the King's English?

A: I will.

When the Detection Club first started, it held three yearly meetings: two at the Garrick Club, for dinner and conversation, and the third at the Café Royal, where the annual initiation rites were held for those members invited to join. It still exists, currently boasting among its living members Ian Rankin (1960–) and Val McDermid (1955–). In the 1930s the original members collaborated on a series of crime novels together, which are still in print.

Chesterton himself was a born and bred Londoner (his original house, in Campden Hill in Kensington – 11 Warwick Gardens – bears a blue plaque). He was a man who loved London from top to bottom, declaring:

> A city is, properly speaking, even more poetic than the coun-tryside, for while Nature is a chaos of unconscious forces, a city is a chaos of conscious ones . . . The narrowest street possesses, in every crook and twist of its intention, the soul of the man who built it.

Chesterton was also quite unusual. Whereas Father Brown was tiny, with 'a face as round and dull as a Norfolk dumpling', Chesterton was a glowering six foot four and weighed twenty stone; he dressed in a cloak, a crumpled hat, and carried a swordstick wherever he went. (A similar stick made a lethal appearance as the killer's weapon in 'The Oracle of the Dog'.)

Yet another Golden Age riff on Sherlock Holmes's personality and peculiarities came in the form of Lord Peter Wimsey, Dorothy L. Sayers's debonair detective. As his name suggests, he is more frivolous than rational, while his address at 110a Piccadilly (a deliberate play on 221b Baker Street – these days it's the Park Lane Hotel) declares a life dedicated to luxury as much as to the temple of the mind. Yet while Wimsey likes to project an idle man-about-town image – and although Sayers claimed she modelled him on Fred Astaire and Bertie Wooster – he is a fiercely intelligent sleuth, who solves endless crimes over eleven novels and two volumes of short stories.

Wimsey is also fun, living in a world of chesterfields, log fires and early folio Dantes. He lunches at the Ritz (wearing, always, a 'topper'), buys wraps from Liberty and suits from Savile Row. He eats marma-lade from Fortnum's and, when at home, likes to have Bach playing gently on the gramophone.

It was wish-fulfilment that led Sayers to forge such an agreeable life for her hero. She loved to have the wealthy detective fritter his

money away on fine living in London: 'After all, it cost me nothing,' she said, explaining how, when she started writing, she disliked
her poky London lodgings – and that giving her beloved character
a sumptuous apartment made her feel better. When her 'cheap rug'
developed threadbare holes, she ordered a special 'Aubusson carpet'
for Lord Peter. When she had no money to pay her bus fare, she presented him with 'a Daimler double-six . . . [and] had him drive it all
over town'.

It's easy to see why Sayers needed cheering up in those early
days. She'd taken a flat in Bloomsbury at 24 James Street, in a neighbourhood swimming with highbrow, image-conscious bohemians
(including her lover, the joyless Imagist poet John Cournos,
1881–1966), but found the area, and above all the people, cold and
unwelcoming. The local avant-garde didn't like her; she wasn't rich;
her love life wasn't going the way she wanted; and she didn't like her
job. That said, she did have several successes at work. She was employed
at S. H. Benson's advertising agency on Kingsway from 1922 to 1931
and worked on projects for Colman's Mustard and Guinness, coming
up with the famous slogans 'Guinness is good for you' and 'It pays to
advertise'. She would later disguise the agency as 'Pym's Publicity' in
her novel *Murder Must Advertise*, describing her boss as a man whose
job is to tell 'plausible lies' for money.

Sayers wasn't against earning a crust herself: she wrote the Wimsey
novels with money in mind, and set about her creation in a busi-
ness-like fashion. Part of the inspiration for her famous character came
from scouring the London newspapers, trying to get a sense of what
people enjoyed reading about and discovering that they liked (i) detectives, and (ii) the aristocracy. That's not to say that the character
should be seen as an entirely cynical creation. Sayers loved him and
obsessed about him so much that she said she sometimes mistook him
for being real.

Agatha Christie (1890–1976), the undisputed queen of the Golden
Age, had similar experiences with her most famous creation, Detective
Hercule Poirot. She insisted that she actually 'saw' Poirot twice: once

on a boat in the Canary Islands and once in the Savoy.

Unlike Sayers, however, Christie loathed her hero. She said that he was a 'detestable, bombastic, tiresome, egocentric little creep', and she regretted that she couldn't kill him off because the public loved him so much. She disliked him to the point that when she was paid to adapt four Poirot novels to the West End stage, she dropped him from the script completely. Yet still, Poirot starred in thirty-three novels after his first appearance in 1920, in *The Mysterious Affair at Styles*. For most of the time, he lived in London. He arrived there in the first novel, living at 14 Farraway Street, and then moved to 56b Whitehaven Mansions (in another tribute to Holmes), and stayed in the capital until 1932, when he retired to Kings Abbot to grow marrows for a year – before realizing that his withdrawal was absurd, and getting back in the saddle and back to Whitehaven Mansions.

Agatha Christie herself regarded Devon as her home – although she kept various apartments around London for most of her life (the longest period was spent at 58 Sheffield Terrace, from 1934 to 1941). She also made her mark on London on the West End stage. She was as successful a playwright as a novelist, adapting several of her detective novels for the London theatres, as well as writing *The Mousetrap*, a murder mystery play which has run continuously since its premiere at the Ambassador's Theatre on 25 November 1952, and has racked up over 26,000 performances. In 1957 *The Mousetrap* broke the record as the longest-running play ever in the West End (Christie was herself convinced that it would last no longer than a year), and Noël Coward

Agatha Christie's favourite London hotel was the Savoy, where she ate regularly. When *The Mousetrap* became the longest-running play in London, her publishers threw a party for her there, with 1,000 guests. Christie, who didn't much like the spotlight, called the evening 'Savoy hell' – which was further inflamed when a porter failed to recognize her and wouldn't let her in.

sent her a telegram reading: 'Much as it pains me I really must congratulate you.'

When Christie died on 12 January 1976, the West End theatres dimmed their lights for one hour in her memory, and there is now a memorial to the writer near to Leicester Square Tube, at the junction of Cranbourn Street and Great Newport Street, in the heart of Theatreland. But possibly the greatest tribute was paid on 6 August 1975 when Hercule Poirot became the first (and last) fictional character to get a front-page obituary in *The New York Times*. This was after Christie published *Curtain*, the novel (actually written during the Second World War, in case events in Europe caused her to bring the series to an abrupt end) in which her Belgian super-sleuth solved his last crime – and laid down his life in the process. 'Nothing in his life became him like the leaving of it,' declared the newspaper – quoting Shakespeare, whom Poirot had himself so frequently misquoted during his illustrious career.

Christie's *At Bertram's Hotel* takes as its model Brown's Hotel, a London institution with a fine literary heritage in and of itself: it was opened by Byron's former valet a few years after the poet's death, in 1837 (and on Albemarle Street, the same road as Byron's publisher). You can still go there and tuck into an afternoon tea very similar to the one Miss Marple eats.

By the time Christie died, the Golden Age of detective fiction was long past. Even so, London has still had its moments. In the 1960s, P. D. James's (1920–2014) Adam Dalgleish liked to roam Soho, all the while calling it the 'nastiest' and 'most sordid' crime nursery in Europe. Ian Rankin's (1960–) supremely gruff Inspector Rebus visits Hackney on assignment from Edinburgh in *Tooth and Nail*. Philip Pullman's (1946–) daring teenager Sally Lockhart finds herself involved in a number of mysteries around Victorian London, taking in the opium trade in

Wapping and dodgy goings-on at the London docks. But it's hard not to feel that there's no champion crime-fighter in town any more – and that maybe, as a result, it's all the easier to commit murder most horrid . . .

KEY ADDRESSES

New Scotland Yard, 35 Victoria Embankment, SW1A (Tube station: Westminster)

The Sherlock Holmes Museum, 221b Baker Street, NW1 (Tube station: Baker Street)

The Langham Hotel, 1c Portland Place, W1B (Tube station: Oxford Circus)

Simpson's-in-the-Strand, 100 Strand, WC2R (Tube station: Covent Garden)

Park Lane Hotel, 110 Piccadilly, W1 (Tube station: Piccadilly)

Florin Court (Whitehaven Mansions), 6–9 Charterhouse Square, EC1 (Tube station: Barbican)

RECOMMENDED READING

Agatha Christie, *At Bertram's Hotel*
Wilkie Collins, *The Moonstone*
Arthur Conan Doyle, *A Study in Scarlet*
Philip Pullman, *The Ruby in the Smoke*
Ian Rankin, *Tooth and Nail*
Dorothy L. Sayers, *The Five Red Herrings*

CHAPTER TEN

. . . AND PUNISHMENT

The companion of crime is, as Dostoevsky (1821–81) assured us, punishment. For every Sherlock Holmes and friend of Scotland Yard in literary London, there's a character who has ended up on the wrong side of the law. And while many writers have been celebrated and publicly feted, plenty too have been disgraced, pilloried and incarcerated.

Thomas More (1478–1535), the author of *Utopia*, ended his days in the Tower of London. His last request was that the axeman mind his beard – because, he said: 'that has not committed treason'. The beard, and the head that wore it, were afterwards displayed on London Bridge.

The adventurer and poet Sir Walter Ralegh (1554–1618) was imprisoned in the Tower between 1603 and 1616, before being released to go on an unsurprisingly unsuccessful expedition to find Eldorado and finally getting the chop at the Palace of Westminster in 1618.

Even such is time, that takes in trust
Our youth, our joys, our all we have,
And pays us but with earth and dust;
Who, in the dark and silent grave,
When we have wandered all our ways,
Shuts up the story of our days:
But from this earth, this grave, this dust,
My God shall raise me up, I trust.

'The Conclusion' – a poem Ralegh is thought to have finished
shortly before his execution in 1618

Ralegh was also imprisoned in the Marshalsea, in Southwark, in 1580 after being convicted of 'fray beside the tennis court in Westminster'. It sounds like fun, but actually he'd been ambushed by Edward Wingfield, who had been commissioned to murder Ralegh by the Earl of Oxford . . . partly because Ralegh had refused to help the Earl to carry out a similar assassination attempt on the poet and playwright Sir Philip Sidney (1554–86).

A few hundred years later, the same prison famously played host to Charles Dickens's father, John Dickens, who was sent there for three months after failing to repay a baker friend a loan of £40. Some of the most famous passages in *The Pickwick Papers* were directly inspired by Dickens's father's imprisonment, although instead of to the Marshalsea, Dickens sent Mr Pickwick to the Fleet Prison for refusing to pay up for a lawsuit.

The Fleet was also briefly graced by the future Dean of St Paul's, John Donne, who was thrown into jail for marrying a minor in 1601. John Cleland (1709–89) was imprisoned there too – for debt in 1748 – and spent his time writing *Memoirs of a Woman of Pleasure* (aka *Fanny Hill*).

That other famous woman of pleasure Moll Flanders was actually born in a London prison, only this time more literally – if you believe Daniel Defoe (1660–1731). The author is said to have written his famous novel – full title, deep breath: *The Fortunes and Misfortunes of the Famous Moll Flanders, Etc. Who was born in Newgate, and during a life of continu'd Variety for Threescore Years, besides her Childhood, was Twelve Year a Whore, five times a Wife (whereof once to her own brother), Twelve Year a Thief, Eight Year a Transported Felon in Virginia, at last grew Rich, liv'd Honest and died a Penitent. Written from her own Memorandums* – after visiting the notorious London criminal Moll King in Newgate Prison in 1731.

Defoe knew of what he wrote. He himself did time in Newgate Prison, accused of seditious libel after writing *The Shortest Way with Dissenters* in 1702. He had argued that the best way of dealing with religious dissenters was to banish them abroad and send their preachers to the hangman. He was joking – but plenty took it seriously. The House of Commons had the book burned, put the author in Newgate, and then sent him to the pillory for the last three days of July 1703. To maximize this punishment, each day Defoe was also marched to a different set of stocks (and on the busiest thoroughfares in London): the Royal Exchange in Cornhill, the conduit in Cheapside and Fleet Street near Temple Bar. But instead of rotten fruit, the crowds threw flowers at him, and his friends even used the opportunity to flog more of his pamphlets. Soon afterwards he wrote the poem *A Hymn to the Pillory*. This too was satirical. It didn't land him in jail, but later he did serve another two stints in Newgate thanks to his awkward habit of posting home truths about the monarchy in his pamphlets.

> *But who can judge of Crimes by Punishment,*
> *Where Parties Rule, and L[aw]'s Subservient.*
> *Justice with Change of Int'rest Learns to bow,*
> *And what was Merit once, is Murther now . . .*
>
> Daniel Defoe, *A Hymn to the Pillory*

Newgate appears in plenty of other literary works. In 'The Cook's Tale' in Chaucer's *Canterbury Tales*, Perkyn Revelour lands himself there because of his riotous living. Shakespeare features it in *Henry VI* part I and part III. In *Richard III*, the king indulges his worst vice by arranging the death of the unlucky Duke of Clarence there. He dies of surfeit 'Malmsey'. Which is to say, he is dropped into sweet wine.

Newgate Prison housed many other famous writers before its last cell door banged shut in 1902, including Ben Jonson, Christopher Marlowe, John Milton, William Cobbett and Thomas Malory. Poor Milton, imprisoned for his parliamentarian views following the Restoration of Charles II, had to sit in his cell while his books were burned in the prison yard.

The less famous but perfectly named poet Richard Savage (*c.* 1697–1743) was also sent to Newgate in 1727, after running his sword through the belly of a man called John Sinclair in a tavern brawl. He claimed he enjoyed 'more tranquillity than I have known upwards of twelve month past' while in the prison (or so Samuel Johnson wrote, in *Lives of the Poets*).

Finally, Newgate cemented its position as a literary landmark by inspiring its own genre of literature. *The Newgate Calendar* (a wildly popular published list of executions in the prison, together with a commentary) led to the 'Newgate Novel' – books which expanded on the lives of London criminals, glamorizing and romanticizing their misdeeds. *Oliver Twist* is often regarded as a Newgate novel. Thackeray also wrote a satire, *Catherine*, sending up the fashion, only to find that readers disregarded the satire and read the work as a Newgate novel itself.

The inspiration for many works of literature, including John Gay's *The Beggar's Opera*, William Harrison Ainsworth's *Jack Sheppard*, and, further down the line, Bertolt Brecht's *The Threepenny Opera*, Jack Sheppard was an eighteenth-century petty criminal who entertained the London populace with multiple prison breaks before his execution in 1724. He was so popular that the London authorities outlawed any plays with the name of Jack Sheppard in the title for forty years after his death.

The outraged law featured in more recent literary history in May 1960 when police raided Flat 4, 25 Noel Road in Islington, the home of playwright Joe Orton (1933–67) and his lover Kenneth Halliwell (1926–67). There, the boys in blue found hundreds of pages cut from books belonging to the nearby Islington Library, and knew they had their men.

Orton and Halliwell had been defacing books from the library for months – because, they said, it contained endless shelves of rubbish. They altered the contents page of the *Collected Plays of Emlyn Williams* so that his best-known play *Night Must Fall* was changed to *Knickers*

Must Fall. Another title read simply: *Fucked by Monty.*

Readers were also surprised by a copy of Dorothy L. Sayers's *Gaudy Nights*, which a new blurb explained was the writer 'at her most awe inspiring. At her most queer, and needless to say, at her most crude!' Meanwhile, those picking up her book *Clouds of Witness* were advised to read behind closed doors 'and have a good shit while you are reading!'

Such improvements infuriated Sidney Porrett, one of the librarians, and he had a good idea who the culprits were. 'I had to catch these two monkeys,' he said. 'They were a couple of darlings, make no mistake.' To catch them, he left an officious note on an abandoned car outside their flat, asking the owner to move it. Orton responded, complaining about town hall interference – using the typewriter he'd used to deface the books. The letter was sent to forensics, the type was linked and a search warrant issued. The lovers were sent to Wormwood Scrubs, in Hammersmith, for six months, where, believe it or not, Orton was given a job in the library.

After his release, Orton wrote *Entertaining Mr Sloane* and *Loot* in Flat 4. Sadly, it was also there that he was beaten to death with a hammer by Halliwell, who then killed himself by taking twenty-two Nembutal pills.

Finally, female writers have not entirely escaped the long arm of the law. Diana Mosley (née Mitford) spent some of the war years in Holloway Prison thanks to her fascist leanings. It failed to disturb her approach to life: she liked to say in later years that she never grew *fraises des bois* (wild strawberries) that tasted as good as those she cultivated in the prison garden. Jean Rhys (1890–1979) also briefly ended up there in 1949, after hitting a neighbour.

KEY ADDRESSES

Tower of London, Tower Hill, EC3N (Tube station: Tower Hill)

The Marshalsea, Mermaid Court, Southwark, SE1 is the approximate location of the prison (Tube station: London Bridge)

The Fleet Prison, formerly on Farringdon Street, EC4 (Tube station: Farringdon)

Newgate Prison, Newgate Street and Old Bailey, EC4M (Tube station: St Paul's)

Holloway Prison, Parkhurst Road, N7 (Tube station: Caledonian Road)

RECOMMENDED READING

Daniel Defoe, *Moll Flanders*

Thomas More, *Utopia*

Joe Orton, *Loot*

CHAPTER ELEVEN
CHILDREN AND TALKING ANIMALS

—✺—

I n 1899, Joseph Conrad (1857–1924) published *Heart of Darkness*, a nightmare journey into inner space set in colonial Africa but told from the deck of a cruising yawl sitting on the river Thames. Elusive in meaning, sombre in intent, dense in its prose, it marked the beginning of the modernist era. Soon writers as different as Virginia Woolf and H. G. Wells were experimenting with form and changing the future of literature for ever. But the modernists weren't the only influential ones. Some of the most enduring writing from the early twentieth century was not quite so dense and difficult. This was also a golden age of children's literature in London: an age whose products would reach and inspire millions of eager readers.

In the same year as Conrad unleashed *Heart of Darkness*, Edith Nesbit (1858–1924) put out her first book, *The Story of the Treasure Seekers*. The book was arguably as important as Conrad's, in its own way. Writers like C. S. Lewis (1898–1963) and Arthur Ransome (1884–1967) (see p.119) later credited it with firing their imaginations – and it also marked the beginning of a singularly productive career.

Born at 28 Lower Kennington Lane, in Kennington, Nesbit went on to write over forty more children's books (when she wasn't campaigning for the London-based Fabian Society and also speaking about workers' rights at the London School of Economics; she was a tireless social activist, too). Several of her books featured London prominently, such as *The Phoenix and the Carpet*, where the five children who appear in *Five Children and It* are living back at their family home in

London and discover, in a new carpet which has been bought for their nursery by their mother (from a shop on the Old Kent Road), an egg that hatches into a talking phoenix. Nesbit's most famous novel *The Railway Children* is mainly set outside the capital, but starts off there, before the children have to move away when their father is sent to prison. A 200-metre walking path in Grove Park, south-east London is named Railway Children Walk to commemorate their association with the area.

Soon after Nesbit's first breakthrough, Beatrix Potter (1866–1943) privately published her *Tales of Peter Rabbit*. The blue-coated carrot-thief emerged from his hole in 1901, after his creator had spent long years drawing animals, starting with the small creatures her nurse used to smuggle into her house in Bolton Gardens in Earl's Court (at first to make up for Beatrix's disappointment at not being allowed to go to school). A big publisher soon stepped in to bring Peter to a wider audience, and following its runaway success, Potter left London for the Lake District. But she kept some of the capital in her heart, leaving a generous bequest in her will to the Victoria and Albert Museum – not least because she based the design for one of her most famous creations, the Tailor of Gloucester's jacket, on a coat she saw in the Kensington museum in 1903. She had also borrowed the names of many of her characters, like Mr Nutkin, Mr McGregor and Tommy Brock, from gravestones she used to see while wandering about Brompton Oratory.

Peter Rabbit wasn't the only classic published in 1901. That year also saw the release of Rudyard Kipling's great masterpiece *Kim*. By the time *Kim* came out, Kipling was already an established poet and writer of books for adults and children alike. *The Jungle Book* had arrived in 1894. In 1891 came *The Light That Failed*, a semi-autobiographical novel with a lead character who rented rooms overlooking the Thames near Charing Cross. The author himself lived in a similar spot for two years on 43 Villiers Street. 'My rooms were small, not over-clean or well-kept,' he wrote in his autobiography, *Something of Myself*.

... but from my desk I could look out of my window through the fanlight of Gatti's music hall entrance, across the street, almost on to its stage. The Charing Cross trains rumbled through my dreams on one side, the boom of the Strand on the other, while, before my windows, Father Thames under the Shot Tower walked up and down with his traffic.

TWENTY bridges from Tower to Kew –
(Twenty bridges or twenty-two) –
Wanted to know what the River knew,
For they were young and the Thames was old,
And this is the tale that the River told . . .

Rudyard Kipling, 'The River's Tale'

By the time he wrote *Kim*, Kipling had bought Bateman's, the grand house in rural Sussex where he lived for the rest of his life. But he frequently returned to the capital, most notably when he took ill with a burst ulcer in Brown's Hotel on 12 January 1936, before expiring in Middlesex Hospital in Fitzrovia on 18 January.

Back in 1901, at 100 Bayswater Road, J. M. Barrie (1860–1937) sat writing about a boy who wouldn't grow up, called Peter Pan. The Bayswater address, also known as Leinster Corner, bears a blue plaque and overlooks the fabled Kensington Gardens, where there is now a statue of Peter. Because of its associations with this famous park, it's commonly assumed that the house of the story's Darling family is somewhere nearby. In fact, the Darlings live in a square in Bloomsbury. Barrie later explained that he placed the house there because it was where Mr Roget (1779–1869, of *Roget's Thesaurus* fame) once lived, and 'we whom he has helped to wend our way through life have always wanted to pay him a little compliment'.

Peter Pan himself was inspired partly by the death of Barrie's beloved brother David when he was thirteen, in an ice-skating accident. Barrie's mother had been devastated, but tried to take comfort in the fact that he would never grow up and leave her – an idea whose impact on Barrie couldn't be clearer. More happily, he was also sparked into creativity by the cheerful life at the house of his friends and neighbours Arthur and Sylvia Llewelyn Davies (who lived nearby in Campden Hill Square, Kensington). They had five sons, George, John, Peter, Michael and Nicholas, whom Barrie loved to visit and entertain with stories. (He also had a talent for wiggling his ears and eyebrows.) Barrie took especially to telling George and John tales about their young brother Peter, saying he could fly and riffing on his boisterous personality. Peter was once told off, for instance, for eating too many chocolates. His mother warned him he'd be sick the next day. He ate more, declaring, 'I shall be sick tonight.'

Peter's fictional namesake first appeared in Barrie's novel *The Little White Bird* (or *Adventures in Kensington Gardens*) in 1902, then took centre stage in his 1904 play *Peter Pan, or The Boy Who Wouldn't Grow Up*, in which Peter 'ran away to Kensington Gardens and lived a long long time among the fairies' – and the Lost Boys.

After the play's success, Barrie decided to turn the play into a novel. He brought it out as *Peter and Wendy* in 1911. But by this time, tragedy had struck. Arthur Llewelyn Davies died in 1907, and Sylvia followed him in 1910 – and their boys would have been all too literally lost had not Barrie himself become their guardian. He looked after them generously – but with mixed results. Indeed, by this stage some began to talk of the curse of Jim Barrie, because an alarming number of people he associated with expired (D. H. Lawrence once declared: 'J. M. Barrie has a fatal touch for those he loves: they die'). Some of these tragedies were as public and painful as could be. Barrie was close friends with Captain Scott (1868–1912), for instance, who perished in the ice and snow of the Antarctic in 1912. The explorer wrote to Barrie in London, in the hopeless final hours of his life, 150 miles from his base camp. Barrie carried the letter with him for the rest of his days in his suit pocket. But worse was to come – and this time, to do with the Llewelyn Davies boys. George died in the First World War in 1915. Then, six years later, Michael drowned in an accident in Oxford, at Sandford Lock. John and Nicholas, at least, lived beyond

Barrie's own death in 1929, as did Peter – although he killed himself in 1960, suffering from emphysema and knowing that his wife and three sons had all inherited Huntington's disease.

So much for growing up.

Christopher Robin Milne (1920–96) was another hero of children's fiction who suffered in later life. He complained of the 'toe-curling, fist-clenching, lip-biting embarrassment' of appearing in the books of his father, A. A. Milne (1882–1956), beside the honey-loving bear.

The stories about Pooh began in 1924, on a happier day, when Milne took his wife and small son to the London Zoological Gardens. There they saw an American black bear, much to the young Christopher Robin's delight. Milne's fellow (and notoriously difficult) author Enid Blyton (1897–1968) liked to embellish the story, saying that Milne had told her that the bear and his son had taken an instant liking to each other (which went so far as the bear hugging Christopher and rolling about and pulling each other's ears and 'all sorts of things'), but the less fanciful Milne simply wrote in his diary that his son had taken a shine to the animal. The bear was called Winnipeg, and had been given to the zoo by a Canadian regiment in 1914, when they were called up to fight in the trenches in France. It liked to be fed a spoonful of golden syrup by its keeper, and is now commemorated by a statue at the zoo. Winnipeg's fictional counterpart made his first appearance in the *London Evening News* on Christmas Eve 1925, in a story called 'The Wrong Sort of Bees'. By this time, the Milnes had partly decamped to the country, although they kept up a house at 13 Mallord Street in Chelsea (where Christopher Robin had been born). One day a week Milne would come up to London for a haircut and lunch at the Garrick Club. He loved the latter so much that he made it part-beneficiary to the rights from his books. To this day, breakfast in the Garrick is served in the Milne Room.

Christopher Robin, it's worth noting, lived to a ripe old age – and even Peter Llewelyn Davies had a reasonably good innings before events overtook him, setting up a publisher called Peter Davies, one of whose most notable successes was P. L. Travers (1899–1996), a huge fan of J. M. Barrie who would go on to become a phenomenon in her own right.

Travers (who was born Helen Goff, but changed her name to Pamela Travers at the age of twenty-one) was depicted recently in the Hollywood film *Saving Mr Banks* as a difficult and stiff spinster. In real life she may have been prickly, but she was far more colourful: she had a series of affairs with older men, was openly bisexual and liked to wear trousers at a time when it was frowned on. She was also eccentric in other ways: she tried to adopt her seventeen-year-old maid and was dedicated to mysticism. As well as changing her name in her early twenties, she jumped on a passenger ship from Sydney, bound for Southampton, and proceeded to set up shop in a tiny flat in Bloomsbury, determined to make her fortune as a writer in London. (She liked to say that she turned up with £10 in her pocket and nothing else, but in fact she was financed by respectable aunts.) Soon she was drinking in the bars of Fleet Street and filing copy for the newspapers, and her first book, *Mary Poppins*, came out in 1934.

The magical nanny is thought to be based on Travers's great-aunt Ellie, an Australian spinster who carried a carpet bag, gave her nieces lessons in etiquette, and liked to say, 'Spit spot into bed!' at night. As to the other characters in the book: the Banks family that Mary works for live at 14 Cherry Tree Gardens – a London address which does not, alas, exist. Poppins enthusiasts place it somewhere around the Regent's Park area, though, in the north-west of the city – and an easy commute to the Bank of England, the model for Mr Banks's fictional place of work. There are real locations in there too, however. Best of all is Admiral Boom's house, which is based on Admiral's House in Admiral's Walk, Hampstead Heath. Admiral's House was adapted to a nautical theme in 1791 by the then occupant, Lieutenant Fountain North, who used to fire a cannon from his roof to celebrate royal birthdays. When it came to illustrating *Mary Poppins*, Travers took the illustrator Mary Shepard on walks through Hyde Park in London, pointing out possible models for the Banks children.

Travers went on to write four more Poppins books, garnering

admirers as diverse as T. S. Eliot and Sylvia Plath – and also, of course, Walt Disney. Disney also took a shine to another London-based writer, Dodie Smith (1896–1990), who moved to the capital from Lancashire in 1910, when she was fourteen, and in adult life lived at 19 Dorset Square, NW1 (in between Baker Street and Marylebone). She started writing children's fiction relatively late: *The Hundred and*

Arthur Ransome's *Swallows and Amazons* series is most closely associated with the Lake District and Norfolk, but the author himself did a good part of his apprenticeship in the capital. He arrived in London in 1901 when he was sixteen, taking a low-paying job as an editorial assistant at the failing *Temple Bar Magazine* and lodging on Chelsea's King's Road (on the top floor of a house with 'desolate, curtainless windows'). He would later write a book about his time in the capital – *Bohemia in London* – where he talks fondly of his misspent youth, his strong desire to be part of a trend-setting underground and heady days and nights in Soho cafés.

THE MOORISH This is where Ransome went to listen to 'strange Moorish melodies', and watch men blow smoke through hubbly-bubbly pipes.

LITTLE PULTENEY STREET In the daytime, Ransome liked to walk along this road, eating bananas bought from a barrow, his heart throbbing to the music of an organ-grinder.

MONT BLANC 'Irregulars,' said Ransome, 'of all sorts' dined here. Among them were Joseph Conrad, G.K. Chesterton and Hilaire Belloc.

ROCHES/BEGUINOFS This 'hot little inferno' was 'Bohemia'.

THE DIEPPE and THE PROVENCE Where Ransome enjoyed the pictures as much as the food, the latter featuring frescos on the walls of gnomes swilling beer and tumbling into vats.

One Dalmatians wasn't published until she was sixty years old, in 1956. Before that, she was better known as a playwright, though she'd also tried her hand as an actress, got a job at the upmarket London furniture shop Heal's, and managed the toy department there (and earned a reputation for her wicked temper – she once flung one of the assistants across the china department).

Smith was also a notoriously lazy employee, but a timely (if scandalous) affair with store-owner Ambrose Heal saved her from getting the sack . . . it also meant that she could indulge her love for style and comfort. With the help of Heal's, Smith was able to furnish her flat in the very latest modernist designs. Ambrose even had a line of furniture designed especially for her, a version of which is still on sale today (it's called the 'Dodie' range and is advertised as 'modern art deco furniture').

Dodie, as you might expect, loved dogs to the point of eccentricity. She would deliberately leave out food for the rats and mice in her homes, fattening them up so that her dogs would have better fun catching and eating them. She was inspired to write her famous novel after one of her friends commented that her pet Dalmatian would make a lovely fur coat.

The house that her fictional family – the Dearlys – live in is not specifically located, but Smith does go so far as to say that it's on the Outer Circle in Regent's Park (and has been lent to them because Mr Dearly, who is a financial wizard, has – usefully – wiped out government debt). The Dearlys also walk Pongo and Missus daily in Regent's Park – and nearby Primrose Hill is where Pongo and Missus start the 'Twilight Barking'. Several other parts of the story are based on real life. The real Pongo did once father a litter of fifteen puppies. One of them was stillborn, just like in the book – and as in the book again, Dodie's husband managed to revive it. There's also a theory that Cruella de Vil was based on the American actress and socialite Tallulah Bankhead (1902–68), who lived near to Dodie in the 1920s – and conspicuously enjoyed driving around in a huge Bentley.

Two years after *The Hundred and One Dalmatians* came out, the world was introduced to Paddington Bear by Michael Bond (who was born in 1926 and still lives in London at the time of writing, not far from Paddington Station). Bond has said that Paddington was inspired by childhood memories of watching children being evacuated from London: they would crowd the stations with labels around their necks, their possessions in tiny suitcases. He is also based partly on Bond's

Buckingham Palace appears in many children's books. A. A. Milne famously sent Christopher Robin there with Alice to watch the changing of the guard. The BFG also visits with Sophie in Roald Dahl's wonderful novel. Even Peppa Pig meets the queen, in – yes – *Peppa Pig Meets the Queen*.

father (who, Bond says, was charmingly 'impractical'), and partly on a lone teddy bear that Bond saw in Selfridges on Christmas Eve in 1956. He bought the bear as a present for his wife and wrote the first book in ten days.

Another character in the *Paddington* series is also based on Bond's war-time experiences: Mr Gruber, a Hungarian refugee and Paddington's great friend, runs an antique shop on the Portobello Road. He was inspired by Bond's time at the BBC Monitoring Unit in Caversham, which was staffed almost entirely by Russian and Polish people.

Many other London locations feature prominently in the *Paddington* series. In one book, Paddington takes a trip to Buckingham Palace, to watch the changing of the guard. At Christmastime, he and the Browns and Mr Gruber go to see the Christmas lights on Oxford Street, and also visit Westminster Abbey (there, Mr Gruber points out a stained-glass window which shows a picture of Dick Whittington's cat). Paddington gets taken as a birthday treat to the Dorchester (the 'Porchester'), where he alarms the staff by ordering marmalade sandwiches and custard. They go to listen to an outdoor concert in Hyde Park (Schubert's *Unfinished Symphony*, which Paddington sets about trying to finish). There's another visit to a certain 'waxworks museum', with a chase through the Chamber of Horrors. And there's a Paddington book of London – where, among a tour of all the classic spots, Paddington wishes that he were an assistant in Fortnum & Mason's marmalade department.

Finally there is Paddington Station, where the bear is first found, sitting on a suitcase with a note attached to his coat reading 'Please look after this bear: Thank you.' These days, at Platform 1, you can find a bronze statue of the very polite bear under the clock, and also buy a gift from the world's only Paddington Bear shop.

Paddington Bear's adventures have sold over 35 million copies worldwide and have been translated into twenty languages, and yet Paddington is no longer the station in London with the most famous literary associations. It's from King's Cross that Harry Potter sets off to school on the Hogwarts Express. Specifically, from Platform 9¾ – as millions and millions of children and adults around the world know full well. King's Cross these days has its very own sign for Platform 9¾, as well as a dedicated shop. J. K. Rowling (1965–) also features London in the series when Harry visits the zoo in Regent's Park in *Harry Potter and the Philosopher's Stone*, and discovers that he can talk to snakes. The Leaky Cauldron pub, alas, is harder to find, although many place it on Charing Cross Road. Diagon Alley, which it leads onto, is sometimes said to have been inspired by the pedestrianized Cecil Court. Close to Leicester Square, and the only court in London to have purely Victorian shop fronts, it certainly looks the part. London turns up in myriad other ways, too – when Hermione, Ron and Harry have to disapparate from Fleur and Bill's wedding, they do so to Tottenham Court Road. Ten Downing Street also makes a cameo appearance in *Harry Potter and the Half-Blood Prince* when the

There is another London location in the *Paddington* series: 32 Windsor Gardens, where the Browns – and the lovable bear – live. And there is an *actual* Windsor Gardens in London, too; it's off the Harrow Road, between Notting Hill and Maida Vale. If you go there, however, you'll only find a very unprepossessing street – and no number 32, because there isn't one. The street bears a relation to Paddington only in terms of its name; if you want a closer approximation, it might be better to head to Chalcot Crescent in Primrose Hill, where the recent movie was filmed.

Minister of Magic appears there to talk to the Prime Minister (partly to explain why odd things have been happening across the country ... such as the collapse of the Millennium Bridge across the Thames). He also visits one other station: Paddington – thus bringing this paragraph full circle.

KEY ADDRESSES

Leinster Corner, 100 Bayswater Road, W2 (Tube station: Bayswater)

Kensington Gardens, Princes Square, W2 (Tube station: Bayswater)

London Zoo, Regent's Park, NW1 (Tube station: Camden Town)

13 Mallord Street, SW3 (Tube station: South Kensington)

Admiral's House, Admiral's Walk, NW3 (Tube station: Hampstead)

Heal's Store, 196 Tottenham Court Road, W1T (Tube station: Goodge Street)

Regent's Park, NW1 (Tube station: Regent's Park)

Selfridges, 400 Oxford Street, W1U (Tube station: Bond Street)

Paddington Railway Station, Praed Street, W2 (Tube station: Paddington)

RECOMMENDED READING

J. M. Barrie, *Peter Pan*

Rudyard Kipling, *Kim*

A. A. Milne, *Winnie-the-Pooh*

J. K. Rowling, *Harry Potter and the Philosopher's Stone*

Dodie Smith, *The Hundred and One Dalmatians*

P. L. Travers, *Mary Poppins*

CHAPTER TWELVE

MODERNISTS AND VORTICISTS

—〰—

A long with the raising of women's hems, the advent of suffragettes and the emergence of a new type of music called jazz, another revolution was taking place in the written word. As the old nineteenth-century certainties gave way at the turn of the twentieth century there came modernism – a new philosophical and literary movement which, among other things, rejected realism in favour of experimentation with form. Modernists believed that every story that could be told had been told already. In order to create something different, they had to use innovative forms of writing. Ezra Pound (1885–1972) told them to 'make it new' – and so they did.

Modernism had already hit a few highpoints by the end of the nineteenth century with books like *Heart of Darkness*, but it burst into the stratosphere round about the time a young T. S. Eliot moved from Oxford to London, aged twenty-five, in 1915. There was nowhere better to make it new than London, still the workshop of the world, the great smoky city, whose thronging ports, factories and warehouses flung out new technologies to every corner of the globe. He finished his first classic poem, 'The Lovesong of J. Alfred Prufrock' – with its vision of London's half-deserted streets, one-night cheap hotels, and looming yellow fog – within a year of hitting the capital.

A few years later, in 1922, the 'unreal city' also formed the setting for Eliot's great masterpiece *The Waste Land*, as well as some gloriously miserable lines about death undoing the crowds flowing over London Bridge.

It would be absurd to doubt Eliot's talent or avant-garde credentials – but his position at the forefront of the difficult and edgy modernist movement would have amazed many of his neighbours and colleagues in London. He may have been a poet by night, but for the early part of his career he worked by day at Lloyd's bank in the City, an unassuming, smartly dressed figure who claimed he needed the regularity of the nine-to-five routine to get him into a poetic state of mind.

Nor was he a typical bohemian. No wild parties and late nights for Eliot. Between 1916 and 1920, when he lived at Crawford Mansions in Marylebone, he in fact claimed to be tormented by noise. There was a pub near his flat, and two noisy sisters in the same block used to bother him – so much so that he complained to his landlord. 'Well you see sir, it's their artistic temperament,' came the reply. 'We ordinary folk must learn to make allowances for artists.'

After that Eliot moved to Burleigh Mansions on Charing Cross Road. There, he did at least receive a few visitors and even host an occasional party. When Virginia Woolf saw him at home in 1922, she came back saying, 'I am not sure that he does not paint his lips.' Later on in the same year, Clive Bell (1881–1964) told Woolf's sister Vanessa (1879–1961) that Eliot had also taken to painting his face green. It was clearly a habit that stuck because when Osbert Sitwell paid him a visit five years later, he was surprised to see a dusting of 'green powder' on his cheeks, 'pale – but distinctly green, the colour of a forced lily-of-the-valley'. Sitwell added, 'I was all the more amazed at this discovery because any deliberate dramatisation of his appearance was so plainly out of keeping with his character, and with his desire never to call attention to himself.'

Osbert Sitwell was a member of the Sitwell clan, along with his brother Sacheverell (1897–1988) and sister Edith, all of them fixtures on the London scene of the early twentieth century. Edith, who was startlingly thin, six foot tall, and had features similar to Elizabeth I, would appear from her shabby flat in Pembridge Mansions, Bayswater (a meeting place for writers) decked out in medieval gowns, gold turbans and a plethora of rings. 'Like a high altar on the move,' according to her neighbour the writer Elizabeth Bowen (1899–1973). The jury is still out on whether Edith's series of abstract poems, *Façade*, is an experimental masterpiece or mere doggerel. When it was performed as a 'live entertainment' in the Aeolian Hall, London, on 12 June 1923, to a musical accompaniment by William Walton, Edith screeched some of the passages through a megaphone (this itself thrust through a muslin curtain). It was a *succès de scandale*, with one headline running: 'Drivel That They Paid To Hear'. Evelyn Waugh, Virginia Woolf and Noël Coward were among the audience. Coward walked out.

No one was sure about Eliot's make-up, either. Perhaps it was about fomenting the poetic mood. Perhaps Eliot was struggling to fit in and show he was a poet as well as a stuffy old bank clerk. (This sort of make-up was quite popular at the time, and the author of *Nightwood*, Djuna Barnes (1892–1982) had taken to parading around London in yellow face paint and a voluminous black cape.) Or perhaps he just liked it. Anyway, whatever he was doing, it worked. His poetry from this period is among the best he ever wrote. And as well as face paint, and the architecture and atmosphere of London, Eliot owed a good part of this creative flowering to the fact that he met Ezra Pound in the capital.

While Eliot only wore his green make-up in private, Ezra Pound went out in public dressed, according to that other modernist genius Ford Madox Ford (1873–1939), in green trousers, hand-painted tie and a purple earring. Ford often saw Pound at 80 Campden Hill Road in Kensington, the house of Violet Hunt, who hosted frequent literary soirées for aspiring writers. Ford and Pound also used to play tennis there, and would astonish onlookers with their fierce competitiveness and disregard for conventional rules. Brigit Patmore (1882–1965), a

> Eliot moved into Crawford Mansions with his first wife, Vivienne, after a three-month whirlwind romance. The 'Hurry up please, it's time' in *The Waste Land* comes from their neighbourhood pub there, the Larrik.

member of Hunt's circle, remin-
isced that the two appeared more
concerned about springing at each
other's throats than at the ball – and
that no one could ever umpire for
them. Ford declared that playing
against Pound was like 'playing
against an inebriated kangaroo'.
Pound, in return, called Ford
'Forty mad-dogs Whoofer'.

The strange scene was
generally topped off when
the two men went inside Violet
Hunt's house for a post-match
drink, and Violet's parrot began
to scream, 'Ezra! Ezra!' – said to be the only words it knew ...

In focusing so relentlessly on Pound, the parrot did no worse
than many later critics, but Ford too is more than worth a place in
the canon. His 1915 novel *The Good Soldier* is an immortal classic.
Equally memorable is the tetralogy of books he put out between
1924 and 1928 under the title *Parade's End*. One critic said the latter was 'as modern and as modernist as they come'. Admittedly that
was Ford himself, but don't let that put you off. They are wonderful
books – and full of references to London, where the awkward hero
Christopher Tietjens ('the last Tory') is a government statistician and
member of the establishment. His wife Sylvia is a socialite, frivolous,
ill-tempered, and made all the more so by the uncouth literary parties her husband encourages her to attend. They are full of 'horrible
geniuses', she shouts at him, after one. 'There was a man like a rabbit
who talked to me about how to write poetry ... I never knew a
beastlier atmosphere.' Ford must have enjoyed writing that.

Ford wasn't Pound's only rival in the capital. While Ezra lived
on Holland Place (also in Kensington), the poet challenged another
poet, Lascelles Abercrombie (1881–1938), to a duel for suggesting

Prufrock was recommended to *Poetry Magazine* in Chicago by Ezra Pound after the poem was rejected by Harold Munro (1879–1932), the influential Londoner who ran both *Poetry and Drama* – one of the best-regarded of the new wave of journals – and the Poetry Bookshop at 35 Devonshire Street in Bloomsbury (now Boswell Street). Munro, who had published Ezra Pound's seminal modernist anthology *Des Imagistes* in 1914, and was sacked from the Poetry Society's *Poetry Review* for his 'liberality towards experimentalists', said Prufrock was 'absolutely insane'. When the poem finally came out in London in 1915, *The Times Literary Supplement* agreed with him. Their review ran: 'The fact that these things occurred to the mind of Mr Eliot is surely of the very smallest importance to anyone, even to himself. They certainly have no relation to *poetry*.'

that new poets should take inspiration from Wordsworth. 'Stupidity carried beyond a certain point becomes a public menace,' said Pound. Abercrombie was briefly worried, as Pound was an expert fencer – until he realized that the person who is challenged has the right to choose weapons. He suggested to Pound that they should fight with unsold copies of their books. Pound dissolved in laughter and the threat blew over.

The equally volatile writer and painter Wyndham Lewis (1882–1957) – strictly speaking a 'Vorticist': a believer in geometric forms rather than landscape and nudes in painting – was also prone to waving weapons around. The society heiress Nancy Cunard – who liked associating with the risqué denizens of Bloomsbury and Fitzrovia – once made the mistake of inviting her lover Wyndham to one of her grand luncheon parties in Mayfair. Edward Windsor, then the heir to the throne, was there (apparently he was eager to meet some of the 'fashionable new writers'), and mayhem ensued when Wyndham appeared waving a pistol.

Such scenes were the exception. More often, modernists were

notable for how much they supported each other. Or, possibly more accurately, how much support Ezra Pound gave to many of them.

Elsewhere, aside from Eliot, one of Pound's most notable pro-tégées was Hilda Doolittle (1886–1961) – H.D., as she was known – an American who moved to London in 1911. She was cham-pioned by Pound soon after her arrival, and lived in an open marriage with the poet Richard Aldington (1892–1962) in Blooms-bury's Mecklenburgh Square. (Until, that is, she ran off with the wealthy English novelist 'Bryher' – Annie Winifred Ellerman (1894–1983) – who wore her hair in a bob, liked to dress in ancient Greek clothes, and subsidized many of the new generation, including James Joyce (1882–1941) and Edith Sitwell.)

Together, H.D., Pound and Aldington formed their own gang, the 'Imagists'. Hilda started calling herself 'H.D. Imagiste' after an after-noon conversation with Ezra Pound in the British Museum tea room, where he sat editing one of her poems. She was also close friends with Dorothy Richardson (1873–1957), the London author and writer of *Pilgrimage*, a thirteen-book sequence which is regarded as one of the great (and greatly neglected) classics of modernism.

Like Eliot, Richardson had a day job. She worked as a receptionist in a Harley Street surgery, lived in Woburn Walk, Bloomsbury, and was

One of the new generation's best methods of literary appreciation was to publish each other's work. The modernist era was a golden age for outré journals and magazines with tiny circulations, all published in London, and ranging from Ezra Pound's *The Egoist* (watchwords: 'Recognise no taboos'), which published parts of *Ulysses*, to T. S. Eliot's *The Criterion* (its first-ever issue featured *The Waste Land*) and Ford Madox Ford's *The English Review* (the journal that launched Jean Rhys and D. H. Lawrence). It was from magazines like these, people said, and their eager editors, that the new tenets of modernism 'seeped like a gas to the rest of London'.

desperately poor. She lived for a time on a daily cup of coffee and a bread roll from the Aerated Bread Company (ABC) Café, off Leicester Square. This poverty came in spite of her groundbreaking writing. It was in relation to Richardson that May Sinclair first applied the phrase 'stream of consciousness' to literature, in a *TLS* review; and when *Mrs Dalloway* was reviewed in 1924 it was described as 'extending the method of Miss Dorothy Richardson'.

> **'In people's eyes, in the swing, tramp, and trudge; in the bellow and the uproar; the carriages, motorcars, omnibuses, vans, sandwich men shuffling and swinging; brass bands; barrel organs; in the triumph and the jingle and the strange high singing of some aeroplane overhead was what she loved; life; London; this moment of June.'**
>
> Virginia Woolf, *Mrs Dalloway*

Mrs Dalloway was just one among many modernist masterpieces produced in London in the mid-1920s, although by this time Pound, the former guiding light of the scene, had left. In 1920 he had declared, 'there is no longer any intellectual life in England' and moved to Paris. Ford Madox Ford soon followed him, to found the

They aren't normally associated with the city, but two other titans of modernism, Samuel Beckett (1906–89) and James Joyce, both spent time in London. Beckett lived at 48 Paultons Square, Chelsea, in 1934, while Joyce had set up shop at nearby 28 Campden Grove a few years earlier, in 1931. For Beckett, although he didn't like the city much, the time in London was useful. He wrote his first novel, *Murphy*, while living in Chelsea (in fact it is set in London). For the Joyces, the relocation was meant to be permanent, but Joyce hated Kensington and the area so much that he took to calling it 'Campden Grave', and they both soon fled back to Paris.

Transatlantic Review. T. S. Eliot, at least, remained. From 1925 onwards he was most often to be found working diligently and for long hours in the Russell Square offices of Faber & Faber – possibly hoping to escape his home life, which was beset by the illness of his first wife, Vivienne.

Poor Vivienne, increasingly unstable by then, took to alarming her husband by appearing at book launches (sometimes in the uniform of Mosley's blackshirts) and also haranguing the receptionists at his work, demanding to see him. In 1934 she even sent an advert to *The Times*: 'Will T. S. Eliot please return to his home, 68 Clarence Gate Gardens which he abandoned sept 17th 1932.' In 1938, after being found wandering the London streets in the early hours of the morning (and saying, reportedly, that Eliot had been beheaded), she was institutionalized. She died in 1947, leaving Eliot free to remarry, which he did in 1952. This was to Valerie Fletcher, his secretary, and they soon moved into 3 Kensington Court Gardens. They occupied the flat until his death – and the end of an era – in 1965.

KEY ADDRESSES

T. S. Eliot's Flat, Crawford Mansions, 62–66 Crawford Street, W1 (Tube station: Baker Street)

Violet Hunt's House, 80 Campden Hill Road, Kensington, W8 (Tube station: Holland Park)

Faber & Faber, original address: 24 Russell Square, now to be found at 74–77 Great Russell Street, WC1B (Tube station: Russell Square)

RECOMMENDED READING

Joseph Conrad, *Heart of Darkness*
T. S. Eliot, *The Waste Land and other poems*
Ford Madox Ford, *Parade's End*
Virginia Woolf, *Mrs Dalloway*

CHAPTER THIRTEEN

BLOOMSBERRIES AND BACK-STABBERS

—ɯɯ—

Alongside all the modernists and Vorticists in early twentieth-century London, there was another (although frequently overlapping) group of writers defined as much by where they hung out as what they thought. A small region of squares to the east of Tottenham Court Road laid claim to being the intellectual heart of London. The British Museum, the British Library and the University of London were located there – as were many of the most important and impressive writers of the time. The area became so famous that it even gave its name to a literary movement: the Bloomsbury Group.

The Bloomsbury Group was a loose collection of writers and publishers with a wide variety of interests and specializations, but they did have at least one thing in common – an association with the sisters Virginia Woolf and Vanessa Bell.

> 'If ever such an entity as Bloomsbury existed, these two sisters, with their houses on Gordon and Fitzroy Square, were at the heart of it.'
>
> Clive Bell, *Old Friends: Personal Recollections*

The Bloomsbury Group started with Vanessa and Virginia's 'Thursday Evening' salons at their house in 46 Gordon Square, around 1905. These were attended by the Cambridge friends of their brother Thoby Stephen (1880–1906), including Leonard Woolf (later Virginia's husband and a publisher), Lytton Strachey (1880–1932, a noted author), Clive Bell (Vanessa's husband and art critic), David Garnett (1892–1981, writer and publisher), Duncan Grant (1885–1978, painter), John Maynard Keynes (1883–1946, a hugely influential economist and author), and Roger Fry (1866–1934, critic and painter). E. M. Forster (1879–1970), author of *Howards End* and *A Passage to India*, was also a distinguished regular.

The parties were originally quite stiff, formal affairs – right up until Lytton Strachey broke the ice one night by asking whether a stain on Vanessa's dress was semen. After a moment of shocked silence everyone burst out laughing, and according to Virginia: 'All barriers of reticence and reserve went down . . . [After that] the word bugger was never far from our lips.'

The Bloomsberries were in and out of each other's underwear as frequently as they were in and out of each other's houses. At different times, the (happily) married Ottoline Morrell was romantically involved with D. H. Lawrence and the philosopher Bertrand Russell (1872–1970). Lytton Strachey had affairs with John Maynard Keynes and Duncan Grant. Duncan Grant made hay with Keynes, David 'Bunny' Garnett and Vanessa Bell. Leonard Woolf had a great crush on Vanessa Bell before he plumped for her sister Virginia . . . And Vanessa's daughter Angelica was only told on her seventeenth birthday that it was Duncan Grant, and not Clive Bell, who was her father. She then went on to marry David Garnett – without knowing that he'd also been Grant's lover. Small wonder that Dorothy Parker (1893–1967) said: 'They lived in squares, painted in circles, and loved in triangles.'

Soon Virginia married Leonard, and except for a brief period away from the centre, when they lived at Hogarth House in Richmond from 1917 to 1924, they spent almost all of their adult lives in

BLOOMSBERRIES

46 Gordon Square The original meeting place for the Bloomsber-ries' 'Thursday Evenings'.

British Museum (Great Russell Street) If it's open, spend some time in Anthony Pazzini's Reading Room, which Woolf immortal-ised in *A Room of One's Own* and *Jacob's Ladder*

33 Fitzroy Square From where the art critic Robert Fry ran the Omega Workshop.

38 Brunswick Square The house Virginia Woolf shared with her brother Adrian, and planned to turn into a commune for intellectuals.

5 Maison Bertaux at 28 Greek Street, Soho London's oldest French patisserie, where the whole Bloomsbury gang loved to tuck into the cakes.

The Lamb on Conduit Street Here, among other Bloomsbury lu-minaries, T. S. Eliot would sometimes sneak out of his offices at Faber & Faber and enjoy a quiet beer.

Bloomsbury, also living at 29 Fitzroy Square, 38 Brunswick Square, 52 Tavistock Square and 37 Mecklenburgh Square. There they were known to many of their neighbours as 'The Woolves', largely thanks to Virginia's vicious tongue. But they still gathered a wealth of friends and intellectuals around them.

Lytton Strachey lived at 51 Gordon Square from 1909 to 1924. He started out as a literary and theatrical critic, and shocked his mother in 1911 when he decided to grow a beard (she said he looked like a

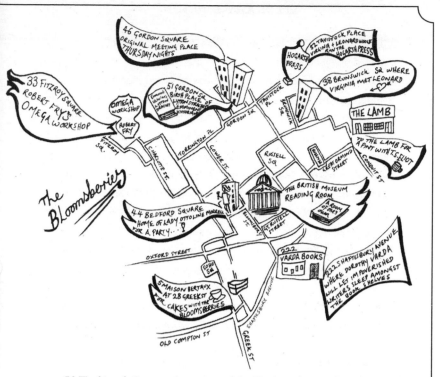

The Bloomsberies

46 GORDON SQUARE ORIGINAL MEETING PLACE THURSDAY NIGHTS

HOGARTH PRESS

52 TAVISTOCK PLACE VIRGINIA + LEONARD WOOLF RUN THE HOGARTH PRESS

38 BRUNSWICK SQ. WHERE VIRGINIA MET LEONARD ♥

33 FITZROY SQUARE ROBERT FRY'S OMEGA WORKSHOP

OMEGA WORKSHOP

ROBERT FRY

51 GORDON SQ. BIRTHPLACE OF LYTTON STRACHEY

THE LAMB

TO THE LAMB FOR A PINT WITH T.S. ELIOT

THE BRITISH MUSEUM READING ROOM

A ROOM OF ONE'S OWN...

44 BEDFORD SQUARE HOME OF LADY OTTOLINE MORRELL FOR A PARTY...

OXFORD STREET

222 VARDA BOOKS

222 SHAFTESBURY AVENUE WHERE DOROTHY VARDA WILL LET IMPOVERISHED WRITERS SLEEP AMONGST THE BOOK SHELVES

5 MAISON BERTAUX AT 28 GREEK ST FOR CAKES WITH THE BLOOMSBERIES

OLD COMPTON ST

GREEK ST

SHAFTESBURY AVENUE

52 Tavistock Square (now part of the **Tavistock Hotel**). Here Virginia Woolf lived with Leonard and, in the basement, ran the Hogarth Press.

44 Bedford Square The London home of Lady Ottoline Morrell, society hostess and patron to the Bloomsbury set.

'decadent poet') and bought a velvet suit. At Gordon Square he also wrote *Eminent Victorians*, the book that made his name. His other claim to fame is his appearance in numerous Bloomsbury novels – as Neville in *The Waves* and St John Hirst in *The Voyage Out* (both by Virginia Woolf), and as Risley in *Maurice* (E. M. Forster). He was also sent up viciously (and in this he was not alone) in Wyndham Lewis's *The Apes of God*.

Other Bloomsbury residents also suffered sharp pricks from their neighbours' pens – none more so than Ottoline Morrell, who was lampooned in over a dozen novels. Ottoline was an eccentric aristocrat (first cousin to the Queen Mother) with flame-red hair who loved to dress in outlandish clothes. She became close to the Bloomsbury Set after meeting Virginia in 1908. Her main house was in Garsington, near Oxford, but she also lived at 44 Bedford Square, where she hosted a weekly salon and first read *Women in Love*, a book where she was caricatured so badly by her ex-lover D. H. Lawrence (in the character of Lady Hermione) that she threatened to sue for libel and never spoke to the author again. Even Virginia Woolf (who loved to slip the knife in) was outraged on her behalf. 'I was so angry I could hardly finish his letters,' she wrote to Ottoline. 'There you are, sending him Shelley, beef tea, lending him cottages, taking his photograph on the steps at Garsington – oft stuffing gold into his pocket – off he goes, has out his fountain pen, and – well.'

Meanwhile, Virginia's sister Vanessa Bell and her husband Clive continued to live in 46 Gordon Square until 1917. Quentin Bell (1910–96), Vanessa's son, recalled in later life how mortified he was that other people had 'normal, sober' front doors, and theirs – in Gordon Square – was painted a 'startling vermilion'. His parents' open marriage hopefully caused him less embarrassment, since it was generally gently accepted by their bohemian neighbours. More frowned upon was John Maynard Keynes, who moved into the Gordon Square house in 1917. Lytton Strachey complained that Keynes was a snob and forever bringing 'dukes and prime ministers' into Bloomsbury – which simply was not on.

E. M. Forster was also a neighbour for a while. Although he preferred to live with his mother in Surrey, and went so far as to call London 'satanic' in *Howards End*, he nevertheless rented a flat as his London base at 26 Brunswick Square in Bloomsbury from 1930 to 1939, and had rooms at what is now the Thistle Bloomsbury Hotel on Bloomsbury Way from 1902 to 1904.

The leading modernist T. S. Eliot, after he quit his banking job, worked at the offices of Faber & Faber in Bloomsbury until his death.

A t Brunswick Square Virginia Woolf had her first breakdown. She suffered horribly and tried to commit suicide by jumping out of an upstairs window. The experience was to inspire her characterization of the shell-shocked hero of *Mrs Dalloway*, Septimus Warren Smith, who – like Virginia – first experiences madness when he hears the birds singing in ancient Greek in Hyde Park. (He also, finally, kills himself by throwing himself from a window.)

He also used to call on the Woolfs, who were his publishers as well as his friends (see p. 155). Once, they invited him round for lunch and an editorial meeting at Tavistock Square. Eliot, who was expecting a decent meal, was put out to arrive and be offered a bottle of ginger beer and a bag of greasy chips.

But the Woolfs were too busy with other things to worry about food and clothes – and most Bloomsberries were famously louche. Henry James went to one of Ottoline Morrell's salons at Bedford Square and was disgusted by the kind of Fitzrovian 'bohemian rabble' she allowed into her home. Their lack of dress code and social niceties bothered him so much that he literally begged her not to be hospitable: 'Look at them. Look at them, dear lady, over the banisters. But don't go down amongst them.' Across town, meanwhile, the diarist James Agate (1877–1947) complained about the dirtiness of the Bloomsbury acolytes, lamenting the invasion of the Café Royal by brigades of 'corduroy trousers . . . with unwashed Bloomsbury fingers'.

In later years, an employee of the Woolfs (and lover of several of their friends), Ralph Partridge, remembered Virginia walking around the offices in the basement 'like a dishevelled angel'. Around this time, in 1939, Virginia and Leonard moved to 37 Mecklenburgh Square, where they lived until the flat was bombed in 1940. As well as T. S. Eliot, the Hogarth Press – the Woolfs' publishing venture – had published Katherine Mansfield, Virginia herself, and the entire translated works of Sigmund Freud (1856–1939). Tragically, when the building was set on fire by incendiaries, all manner of correspondence and manuscript material disappeared. It was the end of an era. Soon after, Virginia Woolf met her own sad end, filling her pockets with stones and walking into the River Ouse. Bloomsbury was never the same again. After the war, prices in the area became too steep for true bohemians to remain there – and that was that.

KEY ADDRESSES

The British Museum, Great Russell Street, WC1B (Tube station: Tottenham Court Road)

46 (and 51) Gordon Square, WC1H (Tube station: Russell Square)

29 Fitzroy Square, W1T (Tube station: Warren Street)

52 Tavistock Square, WC1H (Tube station: Russell Square)

37 Mecklenburgh Square, WC1N (Tube station: Russell Square)

44 Bedford Square, WC1B (Tube station: Russell Square)

26 Brunswick Square, WC1N (Tube station: Russell Square)

RECOMMENDED READING

Michael Cunningham, *The Hours*

E. M. Forster, *Howards End*; *Maurice*

Katherine Mansfield, *Bliss and other stories*

Lytton Strachey, *Eminent Victorians*

Virginia Woolf, *The Voyage Out*; *To the Lighthouse*

CHAPTER FOURTEEN

BOOZERS AND BRIGHT
YOUNG THINGS

—m—

D rinking and literature in London have always gone together,
just like gin and tonic and beer and bonhomie. *The Canterbury
Tales* starts in a London pub (the Tabard; see p. 10). Wine
ran through Shakespeare's plays like lifeblood. Pepys had beer for
breakfast. Romantics loved their blushful vintage. Victorians floated
on port ...

It's perhaps optimistic to try to define any one high watermark for
such a long winding river of booze. Even so, there's no denying that
the sauce had an unusually strong effect on London literature in the
years after the First World War. In the 1920s, authors started lapping
up – and writing about – the good stuff on a scale that was positively
giddying.

One of the most evocative depictions of this period of excess in
London comes in Evelyn Waugh's *Vile Bodies*, which opens with a description of a dinner party where a fox is brought in a cage 'and stoned
to death with champagne bottles'. Waugh goes on to describe endless
parties and debauches around the capital – some of the most notable
in 'Shepheard's Hotel', where the proprietress Lottie has the endearing
habit of charging food and drink to the most wealthy customers (or
to those who annoy her the most) instead of directly to those who
consume it.

Lottie was based on the real life Rosa Lewis (1867–1952), who ran
the Cavendish Hotel on the corner of Jermyn Street and Duke Street,
near Piccadilly. Rosa's eccentricities included refusing to sell any wine

except champagne. She also enjoyed swearing, and declared after she read *Vile Bodies* that Waugh was a 'swine' and that he was one of 'two bastards I'm not going to have in this house' (the other was the gossip columnist Edward Chichester Donegall). Waugh fiercely denied that there was any connection between Lottie and Rosa until Rosa died. Once the risk of his being sued had blown over, he admitted in a 1965 introduction to the book that it was a 'pretty accurate description'.

Waugh – not to mention Anthony Powell (1905–2000), that other great chronicler of London between the wars – had plenty of other real-life material on which to base his fiction, thanks particularly to the presence in the capital of the Bright Young Things.

A set of youngsters from entitled backgrounds sharing a strong desire to buck against convention, the Bright Young Things included the children of some of the oldest and wealthiest families in England (some of whom still appear in gossip magazines today: the Guinnesses, the Mitfords, the Tennants). The group also boasted its fair share of aspiring writers and artists; John Betjeman (1906–84), Cecil Beaton (1904–80) and Henry Yorke (1905–73, pen name: Henry Green) were all BYTs, as well as Powell and Waugh.

Known for carousing around Mayfair, shocking their parents and indulging themselves, the Bright Young Things were especially fond of 'Bring Your Own Bottle' parties, generally held in the house of one or other of their rich buddies. These were almost always based on a theme, and one of the most notorious of them was the Second Childhood Party, thrown in 1929 by Rosemary Sanders at Rutland Gate near Hyde Park and attended by, among others, Nancy Mitford (1904–73), He-Evelyn (Evelyn Waugh) and She-Evelyn (Evelyn Gardner, Waugh's wife; 1903–94). Guests arrived in prams and baby carriages, were given dolls to hold, played on rocking horses in the garden, and were served cocktails in nursery mugs. The *Sunday Express* complained: 'This is the type of behaviour that leads to Communism.'

Equally sick-making (to borrow a Bright Young Thing phrase) was the Bath and Bottle Party held at St George's Swimming Baths on Buckingham Palace Road in July 1928. There, the frivolous aristocrats broke into the municipal swimming pool and proceeded to wreck it, swigging champagne and splashing wildly around as a jazz band played in the background. Finally, and just a few months later, there was the Great Urban Dionysia, a party hosted at 1 Marylebone Street, Oxford Circus, by Brian Howard (1905–58), who is said to be one of the models for Sebastian Flyte in *Brideshead Revisited*. Howard's scheme for the party was that everyone would dress up like Greek mythological figures, and that an appropriate bacchanal would ensue, but despite the anticipation, the night was a washout – 'suburban' was how one gossip columnist put it the following morning. Howard, who was distraught, nevertheless managed to live and party on for another thirty years in the capital (where he also became friends with W. H. Auden, Christopher Isherwood and Edith Sitwell). But he cut an increasingly sad figure around town. 'Drink,' he would later write in his diary, after one party too many, 'has become the No. 1 Problem.'

Drink was also a big problem for Howard's fictional counterpart, Sebastian. One of the funniest – and yet also saddest – episodes in *Brideshead Revisited* comes when he is arrested for drink-driving after filling his boots in The Old Hundredth, a club based at 43 Gerrard Street, in Soho – where Stringham also goes to drink in Powell's *A Dance to the Music of Time* novels.

The Bright Young Things also made good use of plenty of other London locations. Possibly the best-known was the Gargoyle Club on Meard Street. Founded by socialite David Tennant (1902–68), this louche venue was accessed through an obscure Soho alley and then up in a lift. There were Matisse decorations and mirrors said to have been taken from a French chateau. The Gargoyle advertised itself as a place for struggling writers, open day and night, and offering plonk at prices bohemians could afford. The membership was a roll-call of leading writers and associates from the 1920s and 1930s: Dylan Thomas (1914–53), Caitlin Thomas (1913–94), the painter Augustus John (1878–1961), writer Nina Hamnett (1890–1956) and heiress Nancy Cunard (1896–1965) were just a few who attended. A young Evelyn Waugh wrote a cheque to cover his drinking expenses at the Gargoyle (£11, a sizeable amount) which bounced, and caused his non-bohemian father considerable embarrassment when the owners sent him a letter.

There was also the Hambone on 15 Ham Yard, W1, which was established in 1922 as a cabaret club and described in a review as a 'futurist den'. There you could listen to live jazz, and Radclyffe Hall (1880–1943), author of *The Well of Loneliness*, was often seen, wearing men's suits and dancing cheek-to-cheek with her many lovers. As it grew more popular the Hambone graded its membership: artists, authors and journalists paid one guinea; businessmen and society types paid three. A notice on the door read: 'Work is the curse of the drinking classes.' Graham Greene could also be found among the clientele, gathering review material for his short-lived London journal *Night and Day* (which included, as well as reviews and essays, a section on where to go out).

Another venue that tried to support artists was the Crab Tree Club, located at 17 Greek Street, above an R. & J. Pullman leather warehouse. Founded by Augustus John in 1914, this small club billed itself as a no-frills venue serving hard-up creatives and writers. In *Among the Bohemians*, Virginia Nicholson (1955–), grand-niece of Virginia Woolf, describes how its Greek Street premises were reached via a series of staircases, and how drunks and brawlers were frequently thrown down the same stairs. The 'shabby interior', she says, boasted unvarnished wooden tables and chairs. It wasn't always possible to find serving staff – or anyone to pay. But there was a strict rule that anyone turning up in evening dress had to pay a shilling – which went into a fund for food and cigarettes. Jean Rhys (1890–1979) practically lived there, preferring it to her grim rooms over the way, in a boarding house on Gower Street. She would arrive at midnight, dance and drink until dawn, and then have sausages for breakfast before going home to sleep for the day. She later remembered it as 'a decadent place' and said it was 'full of weedy youths drinking absinthe, trying hard to be vicious and hoping they looked French'. It appears in her novel *Triple Sec*.

'Growing old is like being increasingly penalized for a
crime you haven't committed.'

Anthony Powell

The Bright Young Things moved on, but London continued to
swing. The centre of specific gravity moved to Fitzrovia, an area
to the north of Soho bounded by Oxford Street, Euston Road,
Tottenham Court Road and Great Portland Street, which was for
a short period in the 1940s the ground zero for the London avant-
garde. There, a vagabond variety of artists, writers, playwrights,
musicians, poets, journalists and actors could be found swilling beer
and making mayhem into the small hours. You could rub shoulders
with Dylan and Caitlin Thomas, Lawrence Durrell (1912–90),
Nina Hamnett, Aleister Crowley, George Orwell, Augustus John . . .

In *Memoirs of the Forties*, the writer and legendary drinker Julian
MacLaren-Ross (1912–64) recounts an introductory tour around the
bars and pubs of Fitzrovia, guided by J. M. Tambimuttu (1915–83).
Tambimuttu – Tambi to his friends – was a Sri Lankan poet and the
charismatic founder and commissioning editor of the hugely influential
literary journal *Poetry London*, who, after arriving in London in 1938,
quickly made himself at home in Fitzrovia.

Lodging first at 45 Howland Street, then at 2 Fitzroy Street, before
settling at 114 Whitfield Street – where Dylan Thomas once found
the only draft of one of his poems stuffed into Tambi's chamber pot
– Tambi liked to call his drinking tours 'Fitz-rovings', and was an expert on the thriving, bohemian-packed neighbourhood. It's still just
about possible to follow the pub crawl to which he treated Julian
McLaren-Ross - and which you can follow, overleaf, on the listed
walk. As good as this walk might be, Tambi missed out some key pubs
– including the Fitzroy Tavern which, for a while, eclipsed them all.
It may have become a victim of its own success by the 1940s – when
Tambi missed it out – but in the 1930s it was one of the great literary
pubs of London. Most nights throughout the glory years, the Welsh
writer and muse Nina Hamnett could be found there carrying a little

TAMBIMUTTU'S FITZROVIAN PUB CRAWL

(1) THE BLACK HORSE (6 Rathbone Place, W1T)

Now a pub again, after a brief unfortunate stint as a Byron Burger joint, this was once the place that was according to MacLaren-Ross, 'the first to be reached, and usually the last to be visited, entering Rathbone Place from Oxford Street'.

(2) THE BRICKLAYER'S ARMS (31 Gresse Street, W1T)

Also known as the Burglar's Rest because a gang of burglars had once broken in and spent the night there working their way through the stock, this pub was a highlight of Tambimuttu's suggested pub crawl, although little of literary note seems to have happened there. Presumably because everyone was too busy enjoying the beer.

(3) THE MARQUIS OF GRANBY

(2 Rathbone Street, W1T)

T. S. Eliot's favourite pub and reputably a rough place: the haunt of street girls and petty gangsters, and a cruising ground for sailors on leave. Dylan Thomas used to crawl in, hoping to start fights with guardsmen who were there to find gay partners. He also wrote 'The Death of the King's Canary' there.

(4) THE WHEATSHEAF (25 Rathbone Place, W1T)

The pub where Dylan Thomas met his future wife, Caitlin. He laid

tin and collecting contributions from other patrons, to buy her own refreshments. 'Got any mun, dear?' she would ask, or 'You couldn't buy me a drink, could you, love?' Given enough dosh, she would start to tell stories about 1920s Paris; about her time working as a model, hanging out with Picasso, meeting James Joyce, making love to his head in her lap, by way of introduction, and proposed to her. Less romantically, George Orwell once threw up all over the bar. This pub is also, by anecdote, supposed to be the place where Orwell got the idea for the horrible rat sequence from Room 101 in *Nineteen Eighty-Four*, after listening to Gilbert Wood, the famous set designer, talking about his work on a film called *Death of a Rat*.

(5) THE NEWMAN ARMS (23 Rathbone Street, W1T)

This traditional boozer was the model for the 'prole pub' in George Orwell's *Nineteen Eighty-Four* – ironic, given the crowds of local advertising execs who now pile in here for the tasty pies upstairs. In the period that Orwell was a regular, the pub was run by a poet – Joe Jenkins – who is now commemorated with a blue plaque: 'Joe Jenkins, ex-proprietor, poet, bon viveur and Old Git, regularly swore at everyone on these premises'.

(6) THE HIGHLANDER

(Now called The Nellie Dean, 89 Dean Street, W1D)

A late-opening bar to which the artists and drinkers would decamp en masse after the other local bars began to close. 'If there was a unified literary movement in the forties,' said Anthony Burgess, 'it was only in the sense of poets and poetlings moving together from The Wheatsheaf, which closed at ten-thirty, over to the Highlander in Dean Street ...'

Modigliani. The latter, she said, had especially liked her breasts – and she would demonstrate why, pulling off her top and saying, 'You feel them. They're as good as new.'

Dylan Thomas liked the Fitzroy too, and would write poems on beer mats for the prettiest women in the bar. Aleister Crowley was

George Orwell is best known for his austere morality and dedication to socialism, but he also knew how to party. He celebrated *Animal Farm*'s selection by the American Book of the Month Club by drinking absinthe in the Dog and Duck on Bateman Street. He also wrote a famous essay, 'The Moon Under Water', about the ideal pub (based on the Canonbury Tavern in Islington) – a place quiet enough to talk, offering liver sausages on the snack counter, and quality beer served in glasses with handles.

another regular. He was supposed to have created The Kubla Khan No 2 cocktail for the Fitzroy, a potent combination of gin, vermouth and laudanum.

It's also well worth while dropping in on the Duke of York on Rathbone Street – although you may not want a literal recreation of its biggest claim to literary fame. One night in 1943, Anthony Burgess and his wife Lynne were drinking at the Duke of York when a razor gang (the 'Perellis') rushed in. They smashed glasses, threatened the patrons and poured beer on the floor. Burgess's wife complained – which prompted them to demand she drank a significant number of pints herself. She downed them with such aplomb that they paid for them, and offered to protect her from other gangs. The incident was part of the inspiration for *A Clockwork Orange*.

Don't try to emulate the drinking of Dylan Thomas either. You wouldn't keep up. No one in London seemed better at drinking than the Welsh poet – until his tragically early death in 1953 demonstrated that even his cast-iron constitution could only take so much. In happier years, he could often be found drunk (but brilliant) at the BBC's Portland Place studios on Langham Street. Once he fell asleep before doing a live poetry reading and even started snoring. He was woken up two minutes before the broadcast and did a near-perfect reading of 'Saint Cecilia's Day' . . . which he managed with hardly a slur. Less happily from his producer's point of view, he also once stopped his own broadcast, saying, 'Somebody's boring me. I think it's me.'

For a long time Thomas lived in a house at Wentworth Studios (on Manresa Road, in Chelsea) where he had furniture made out of books – although for a short while in the 1930s he also shared a private room at the Eiffel Tower Hotel, 1 Percy Street, with Caitlin Macnamara. When they finally left, Thomas charged the bill to Augustus John, who accused the proprietor of fiddling him: 'I know you cheat me outrageously . . . But £43 for a lunch or two is a bit steep.' The (Austrian) hotelier replied that it wasn't just for lunch: 'Little Welshman with curly hair. He stays two weeks and eat. He says you pay.'

Thomas was also once discovered staggering down King's Road (in Chelsea again) by the cookery writer Theodora Fitzgibbon (1916–91). He was carrying a sewing machine – Fitzgibbon's sewing machine, in fact (Thomas was sleeping on her sofa at the time), which he was trying to sell to buy drinks.

Almost worst of all, in 1953 Thomas left his only, handwritten, manuscript for *Under Milk Wood* in a pub in Soho (some say it was the French House, others the Swiss) before flying to New York. Fortunately, it was found by the aptly named BBC producer Douglas Cleverdon, and the poet's legacy was ensured. Probably in spite of the drink, rather than because of it.

If all that booze has left you with a headache, you may be interested

One of London's best-known drinkers at the end of the twentieth century was the journalist Jeffrey Bernard (1932–97), who was as famous for sitting in the Coach and Horses in Greek Street as he was for writing copy. He often failed to file, and the words 'Jeffrey Bernard is Unwell' would appear instead of his column. He remained unrepentant, saying, 'People often ask me if drinking has ever interfered with my work, to which I always reply, no, it has never interfered with my work, though my work has occasionally interfered with my drinking.'

in one of literary London's finest hangover cures, courtesy of the great P. G. Wodehouse (1881–1975). Jeeves first wins over the affections of Bertie Wooster – and gets a job as his valet – after providing him the 'extremely invigorating' hangover cure of raw egg, Worcester sauce and red pepper.

Many of the pair's subsequent adventures begin at 3 Berkeley Mansions, Bertie's fictitious address on Berkeley Street in Mayfair, or in the nearby Drones Club, which is often thought to be based on Bucks at 18 Clifford Street. Bertie and his friends also enjoy roaming the city. In *The Code of the Woosters*, after enjoying the festivities on Boat Race night a little too much, Bertie gets arrested in Leicester Square for stealing a policeman's helmet. His friend Gussie Fink-Nottle lands in even worse trouble when he plunges into the fountains in Trafalgar Square and earns himself fourteen days in jail in *The Mating Season*.

> **'Percy continued to stare before him like a man who has drained the wine-cup of life to its lees, only to discover a dead mouse at the bottom.'**
>
> P. G. Wodehouse, 'The Amazing Hat Mystery'

Wodehouse himself also managed to get on the wrong side of the law in the capital. After he left Dulwich College school in 1900, problems in the family finances forced young Plum to get a job as a clerk at the Hong Kong and Shanghai Bank (on 9 Gracechurch Street, not far from the Bank of England). Wodehouse later claimed he was always on the brink of arriving late and used to arrive at a sprint, cheered on by other clerks, in order to clock in on time. But the real crunch came when he stole some office paper to write a short story. He was, he said, the 'worst burglar ever to have entered the portals of the Hong Kong and Shanghai Bank'. When the crime was discovered, the head stationer declared that 'only an imbecile' would tear out the first page of a ledger. So he immediately summoned Wodehouse. The writer owned up and was fired after less than a year on the job. Banking's loss is our immortal gain. He soon snagged a column on *The Globe* magazine and started writing full-time, producing many of the finest sentences written in English since Shakespeare held a quill.

KEY ADDRESSES
The Cavendish Hotel, 81 Jermyn Street, SW1Y (Tube station: Green Park)
The Nellie Dean, 89 Dean Street, W1D (Tube station: Tottenham Court Road)
The Fitzroy Tavern, 16a Charlotte Street, W1T 2LY (Tube station: Tottenham Court Road)
The Duke of York, 47 Rathbone Street, W1T (Tube station: Tottenham Court Road)

RECOMMENDED READING
Julian McLaren-Ross, *Memoirs of the Forties*
Anthony Powell, *A Dance to the Music of Time*
Evelyn Waugh, *Vile Bodies; Brideshead Revisited*
P. G. Wodehouse, *The Code of the Woosters*

CHAPTER FIFTEEN

PUBLISHERS AND BOOKSELLERS

—⚍—

' To a lover of books the shops and sales in London present irresistible temptations,' said the historian Edward Gibbon (1737–94). George Orwell pointed out that they offered other benefits too. 'In a town like London,' he said, 'there are always plenty of not quite certifiable lunatics walking the streets, and they tend to gravitate towards bookshops, because a bookshop is one of the few places where you can hang about for a long time without spending any money.'

Orwell would know, as he is one of London's many famous booksellers, having worked in a shop near Camden Town, where he said that having to lug heavy hardbacks day in, day out almost destroyed his love of books.

He might also have noted that the most splendid eccentrics of them all were often the people selling the books. One of the greatest was James Lackington (1746–1815), a forgotten hero of the book trade and a man with a rags-to-riches story to rival Dick Whittington. When he first arrived in London with his wife, he spent his last half-crown on a book, reasoning 'had we bought a dinner, we should have eaten it to-morrow, and the pleasure would have been soon over'. A book, on the other hand – at least, if it was a good one – offered delight that would last the rest of their lives.

As it turned out, Lackington was in luck, and the volume that he and his wife went hungry for – *Night Thoughts* – was indeed fine. An epic poem by Edward Young (1683–1765) on the theme, as its title

suggests, of the hours of darkness, the book remained popular for years – and was later released in an edition illustrated by William Blake in 1797.

By the time this version came out, Lackington had also made his mark. He had come up with the revolutionary idea of selling cheap remaindered stock, determined that reading should be available to the many, not just the few. In 1792 he had saved up enough money to open a huge shop in Finsbury Square, which quickly became known as the Temple of the Muses. It was so big that a mail coach pulled by four horses was driven around the counters at its opening.

This shop was further notable because the publishers John Taylor (1781–1864) and James Hessey (1785–1870) met there, while working behind the desk as booksellers. They would go on to publish John Keats, Percy Bysshe Shelley and Charles Lamb.

John Milton was also first published by a bookseller, Samuel Simmons (1640–87), who flogged books from his house. This was located – as he printed inside his publications – 'next to the Golden Lion on Aldersgate Street'. Simmons is infamous today because he is supposed to have given the blind poet just £5 for *Paradise Lost* in the 1660s and to have promised him another £5 if he sold 1,300 copies. In fact, the deal gave Milton £20 and a share of future earnings – not such bad money, at a time when writers often weren't paid at all.

Less forgivable are the actions of John Murray II (1778–1843), the bookseller-cum-publisher of Lord Byron, among others, who when Byron died in 1824 threw the Romantic poet's diaries onto the fire at his house and offices at 50 Albemarle Street. Murray was concerned that the diary (written by a man who had only recently been driven out of England by the scandal of an affair with his own sister) would further harm the poet's posthumous reputation. By burning it, he deprived generations of readers of what was probably some of the world's greatest literary gossip – and made no difference to Byron's standing, since everyone found out that he shagged his sister anyway.

In happier times, Murray and Byron also started one of London's biggest literary sensations when Murray published the first two cantos of Byron's *Childe Harold's Pilgrimage* in 1812. Available from Murray's bookshop at 32 Fleet Street, the volume sold out in three days – and Byron became the first literary heartthrob. ('Should curiosity prompt you, and should you not be afraid of gratifying it,' one star-struck groupie wrote in a letter – then she would be waiting in London's Green Park at 7 p.m.)

Ten years later, Byron wrote a letter to John Murray at his Albemarle Street offices, pretending to be his own devoted valet, Fletcher. In the letter, 'Fletcher' declared his misery at having to pass on the bad news that Byron was dead. Tragically, just two years later the real Fletcher wrote a very similar letter – only this time, Byron really had died, after contracting a violent fever while fighting for Greek independence at the Gulf of Corinth. 'Please to excuse all defects,' the letter began, 'for I scarcely know what I either say or do ...' Soon afterwards, the grieving Murray was consigning the poet's diaries to the flames.

John Murray sold a commendable number of books – but at a price, and to a well-heeled clientele. More in the tradition of Jack Lackington was Allen Lane (1902–70), the founder of Penguin Books, who decided that the best way to get books to everyone wasn't simply to sell remaindered copies at a cut rate, but actually to publish cheap books in the first place.

Legend has it that Lane came upon the idea for his company while waiting for a train back to London from Exeter, where he had been visiting Agatha Christie. He found himself without reading material and was disgusted by the books available at the station, so there and then decided to publish paperbacks – economically produced books that combined a cheap cover price with fine writing and stylish design. They would be made available in everyday shops like Woolworths, and also in vending machines – 'Penguincubators' – located in train stations.

The company launched in 1935 from the offices of Lane's uncle's firm, The Bodley Head, at 8 Vigo Street, Mayfair (which today has a blue plaque commemorating the company that 'changed the reading habits of the English-speaking world'). No one thought the idea would work. The Bodley Head refused to pay for the venture, and Lane's parents had to mortgage their house to pay Penguin's initial costs. But the gamble came off – the purchase of 63,000 books by Woolworths soon after Penguin set up in 1935 paid for the project. Lane was able to establish Penguin as a separate business, and he promptly abandoned The Bodley Head, moving to the crypt of Holy Trinity Church, on Marylebone Road, around the corner from Great Portland Street Station.

This latter address actually proved vital to Penguin's success, since it was to Great Portland Street Station's toilets that Lane's staff went when they needed (literally) to spend a penny. Lane even gave them extra money to do so. Other eccentric arrangements of the first offices included a fairground slide leading from the street into the crypt for the delivery of parcels. None of this hampered the company's fortunes. By 1936 – just one year on from its inception – Penguin had sold more than a million books.

Not coincidentally, given those pleasing sales figures, another London cheap book operation was set up in 1936 in Henrietta Street, just off Covent Garden: the New Left Book Club. Founded by Victor Gollancz (1893–1967) as an offshoot of his main (and more orthodox) publishing concern, Victor Gollancz Ltd, this subscription service had its origins in Gollancz's desire to revitalize the British political Left and 'help in the terribly urgent struggle for world peace and against fascism'. The club issued a monthly book choice to its members and issued a regular newsletter that itself became a major political magazine. Counting among its early authors George Orwell, Clement Attlee (1883–1967) and Stephen Spender (1909–95), and aiming to break even with 2,500 members, it had almost 40,000 within its first year, and 57,000 by 1939. Over 1,200 book clubs also sprang up over the country to discuss the monthly choices, and it's not too far a stretch to say that the club – and its ethos – helped Labour towards its monumental election victory in 1945.

It wasn't all brotherhood, however. When Gollancz published Orwell's *The Road to Wigan Pier* (a book about working-class life in the north of England), he insisted on writing an introduction disowning middle-class socialists – socialists much like Orwell, in fact, who, Gollancz said, didn't properly understand working-class life. He even later republished *The Road to Wigan Pier*, leaving out the second half, of which he disapproved. Little wonder that Orwell took his next book – *Homage to Catalonia* – to Secker & Warburg (over the road and on to Soho's 14 Carlisle Street) instead.

Gollancz wasn't the only editor who disapproved of George Orwell. From the Bloomsbury offices of Faber & Faber (at 24 Russell Square, a stone's throw from the British Museum), T. S. Eliot condemned the 'Trotskyite' politics of *Animal Farm* and wondered if Orwell actually had 'anything to say'. Such comments may have had something to do with the fact that, after Eliot similarly rejected Orwell's first work – *Down and Out in Paris and London* – back in 1932 ('I regret to say . . . it does not appear to me possible as a publishing venture'), Orwell had taken a swipe at the poet in several of his subsequent books. In *The Road to Wigan Pier*, he went so far as to call Eliot a fascist and a 'damp squib'.

But Eliot also had a number of great successes during his time at Faber – where he worked from shortly after the company's foundation in 1925 until his death in 1965. The first was his decision to publish *Memoirs of a Fox-Hunting Man* by Siegfried Sassoon (1886–1967) in 1928, which was reprinted eight times in six months. Thanks to Eliot, the company also took on other lasting writers like Ezra Pound, Jean Cocteau (1889–1963), W. H. Auden (1907–73) and William Golding (1911–93).

While Eliot was at Faber, he initiated and chaired the 'Book Committee', a long editorial session every Wednesday, where all the directors and editors sat down from 11 until 4 and decided what they would publish. These meetings were enlivened by generous amounts of beer and Eliot's occasional inclusion of spoof reports. Not everyone was welcome, however. Employees of Faber & Faber used to regularly shield Eliot from his estranged wife, Vivienne. They refused to tell her when he was in the office when she turned up at the reception desk, desperate to see her husband.

Some of Eliot's friends were sympathetic to Vivienne's plight, though not Virginia Woolf. The waspish writer observed that the poet wore the poor woman 'like a bag of ferrets around his neck'. Woolf knew Eliot well enough to make these kinds of remarks – not least because she was his publisher. The small press she ran with her husband Leonard, Hogarth Press, was originally founded – on a hand-printing press – to give her something 'congenial to do' and distract her own troubled mind when she wasn't writing.

The Woolfs weren't the first publishers to hand-print in London. That honour goes to that other great pioneer William Caxton, who set up the first printing press in England in a rented shop (exact location sadly unknown) in Westminster in 1476. Between then and his death in 1492 (helped, in a beautiful example of nominative determinism, by a man called Wynken de Worde) he printed over 100 books, including *Le Morte D'Arthur* and *The Canterbury Tales*. Oh – and he helped standardize the English language. Not bad going.

Set up in 1917, the company took its name from the Woolfs' house in Richmond-upon-Thames: Hogarth House (on Paradise Road). The first book was riddled with errors and blotches (it is of course now worth a fortune), but the couple persevered. The press soon took up full residence, in the words of Virginia Woolf: 'creeping all over the house'. Meanwhile, Leonard said, 'We bound books in the dining room, interviewed printers, bookbinders and authors in the sitting room . . . and printed in the larder.'

The Hogarth Press might well have been at the forefront of the avant-garde in the 1920s – but that didn't mean they were in favour of *everything*. In fact, they rejected *Ulysses*, telling James Joyce that the effort required in the typesetting was just too much for their tiny press. In private, Virginia said that the book was 'tedious', 'vulgar', and a load of 'tosh'. Joyce, who never forgave a slight, later took to calling them the 'willy wooly woolfs' in *Finnegans Wake*.

In 1924 they moved back to the centre of Bloomsbury, just around the corner from Faber & Faber, at 52 Tavistock Square. Taking the upstairs rooms as their domestic quarters and devoting the cellar to the press, over the next few years – and on a shoestring – they set about publishing Eliot's poetry, as well as classics by E. M. Forster and Katherine Mansfield.

From amid the horrors of the Second World War, Hitler inadvertently made a significant contribution to London literary life. As the bookshop owner and counterculture expert Barry Miles (1943–) explains in *London Calling*, a good half-dozen of London's most groundbreaking and era-defining independent publishing houses were established in the second half of the twentieth century by European Jews, who had fled to London to escape persecution.

Take Peter Owen (1927–2016), whose original name was Offenstadt and who fled from Berlin in the 1930s. He founded his eponymous press in 1951 in his own house on the Kenway Road in west London, running editorial from the kitchen table. The first editor he employed was the writer Muriel Spark, who he called the 'best bloody secretary I ever had'. She later wrote a novel, *A Far Cry from Kensington*, that drew on her experiences at the eccentric publishers. Owen published an electrifying list, with writers ranging from Paul Bowles (1910–99) to André Gide (1869–1951) and Jean Cocteau, Colette (1873–1954), Anaïs Nin (1903–77) and Hermann Hesse (1877–1962). He also became one of the leading lights of the Swinging Sixties, a period during which his offices were described as a 'psychedelic lair'.

Pay tribute to ghosts of publishers past at Paternoster Row. This street was once the centre of the London book trade, until one night in December 1940, when a bombing raid destroyed 5 million books, as well as the offices of dozens of publishers.

Similarly, André Deutsch (1917–2000) came over from Budapest and was inspired to become a publisher while interned as an enemy alien on the Isle of Man, where he made friends with a European literary editor. André Deutsch Ltd began trading properly in 1952, and among such classics as *Wide Sargasso Sea* and the early works of V. S. Naipaul (1932–2018), he brought out *The Naked and the Dead* by Norman Mailer (1923–2007). UK censorship in those days meant that he was forced to change 'fuck' to 'fug' throughout the novel, but the resulting controversy ensured that the book became a hit, and the fortunes of the company were set.

Deutsch also employed Tom Maschler (1933–2020), who had fled to London from Vienna with his parents, aged six. Maschler went on to put out the Angry Young Men's anthology/manifesto *Declaration*, head Jonathan Cape and become famous in the 1960s as the publisher of *Portnoy's Complaint*, *Catch-22*, and *A Moveable Feast*.

Finally, George Weidenfeld (1919–2016) arrived in London in

1938 from Vienna. Ten years later he co-founded the firm Weidenfeld and Nicholson – and he went on, in 1959, to publish the first British edition of *Lolita*.

After the war, London continued to be the home to big houses like Macmillan and Penguin – but a newer, hipper, chippier breed of publisher also burst onto the scene. Chief among them were John Calder (1927–2018) and Marion Boyars (1928–1999), who changed the face of twentieth-century literature from their offices on 18 Brewer Street, Soho. Steadfast supporters of off-beat writing and the 'nouveau roman', Calder and Boyars published, among others, Henry Miller (1891–1980), Marguerite Duras (1914–96), William Burroughs (1914–97) and Samuel Beckett.

According to *The Uncensored Memoirs of John Calder*, Beckett bonded with his publishing company after a first meeting and an afternoon in a Soho café discussing 'life, its pointlessness, and the cruelty of man to man'.

Calder thrived on controversy, with book-lovers rushing to buy the latest C&B publication 'before it was banned' and queuing up for headline-grabbing events. On one occasion in Edinburgh, a reading was enlivened by a naked young woman . . . wheeled around in a shopping trolley.

In this era many new bookshops catering to the avant-garde sprang up. Better Books opened in 1947, at 92 Charing Cross Road. It was a hang-out for Angry Young Men in the 1950s but came into its own in the 1960s, when it grew so popular that the owner Tony Godwin (1920–76) enlarged the shop, expanding into the buildings around the corner at 1, 3 and 5 New Compton Street. Godwin's somewhat obscure instructions to the interior designer were that he wanted to have books 'floating in a silver mist'. The designer came up with freestanding bookshelves on wheels. They were painted silver and the paint came off on the books. The shelves themselves fell over if anyone leaned on them too hard. But still, the shop was one of the few places in Britain you could pick up a Henry Miller title (Miller was still banned in the UK; Better Books got around this by ordering the books directly from Grove Press's US warehouse, where the staff didn't know the book was illegal). It was also a crucial exchange hub with the 'Beat Generation' City Lights Bookstore, in San Francisco – to the extent that City Lights once sent over a manager to 'bohemianize' Better Books. Once also – and once only – Jeff Nuttall (1933–2004), countercultural poet, 1960s provocateur and all-round renaissance man, gave a reading at Better Books that involved throwing large chunks of raw meat at the audience . . . He otherwise appeared there every Monday and Tuesday from 1966 to 1968 with his 'People Show', a group of performance artists whose remit was to shock and horrify people out of complacency, which involved such spectacles as pulling sopping offal out of a pregnant woman's stomach while screeching violent poetry.

'There is a special peculiar atmosphere to these Better Books functions, a sort of curious mixed atmosphere. Part Quaker, part Anarchist, part decadent. The crowd usually consists of idealistic figures in publishing, up and comings, amiable potheads, one or two celebrities and a rash of kids of all three sexes.'

Jeff Nuttall

In 1965, when Better Books was sold to Hatchards – the oldest bookshop in the city and a decidedly old-fashioned purveyor of signed first editions – the London counterculture went into a tailspin, and it was decided that another bookshop was needed. So it was that late that year the Indica Bookshop was opened, featuring, like Better Books, an exhibition space as well as a shop. Located first in Mason's Yard (off Duke Street, St James's), the bookshop was described as 'a ticket to a magic kingdom' by rock star, journalist and science-fiction author Mick Farren (1943–2013). It also quickly became one of the focal points of Swinging London. Books by William Burroughs, Malcolm X (1925–65) and J. G. Ballard (1930–2009) shared shelf space with LPs by Sun Ra and The Fugs; there were spoken-word records from Ezra Pound and Lenny Bruce (1925–66). The underground newspaper the *International Times* operated from its basement, and upstairs there was a gallery, which hosted the

Hatchards is the oldest bookshop in London – and the UK. It was founded by John Hatchard in 1797 and has been at 187 Piccadilly since 1801. Back then, *The Edinburgh Review* described the clientele as 'a set of well-dressed, prosperous gentlemen, assembling daily at the shop well in with the people in power, delighted with every existing institution and every existing circumstance'.

Patrons have remained upmarket ever since. This is where the royals have shopped for their books from Queen Charlotte onwards (Prince Charles, Prince Philip and the Queen all have accounts there).

There have also been more cerebral visitors. Byron lived just across the road for much of his time in London. Oscar Wilde, meanwhile, favoured Hatchards as his bookshop and bought green carnations (his preferred flower for his buttonhole) from the nearby Royal Arcade. Poignantly, Oscar's wife – Constance Wilde – would later order her copies of *The Ballad of Reading Gaol* from the shop.

Noël Coward was another customer. When he was a teenager, he stole a suitcase from Fortnum & Mason, took it to Hatchard's, and proceeded to fill it up with books. Being caught wasn't enough to put him off – and when he was caught shoplifting on another occasion, he simply said: 'Really! Look how badly this store is run. I could have made off with a dozen books and no one would have noticed.'

show where John Lennon first met Yoko Ono. In 1966, when the shop moved to Southampton Row, co-owner Barry Miles claims that he gave Lennon a copy of Timothy Leary's introduction to the *Tibetan Book of the Dead*. On page 14, Leary (1920–96) offered some helpful advice about turning off your mind, relaxing and floating downstream. It formed the opening lines for 'Tomorrow Never Knows'.

Foyles first opened in 1903 at the home of its founders William and Charles Foyle, before moving to the antiquarian book paradise of Cecil Court in 1904, and then in 1906 to a longer-lasting home at 135 Charing Cross Road. This shop was once listed in the *Guinness Book of Records* for having the most shelf space of any bookstore in the world (upwards of 30 miles). It was just as famous for the fact that it was very hard to find anything on those shelves.

In 1945, the shop was handed down to Christina Foyle, daughter of William. She was responsible for several successful innovations, such as a long-running series of literary luncheons with famous authors. But she also caused a fair bit of chaos. For a long time she refused to install electronic tills. There was instead a convoluted payment system in the shop that made customers queue three times: first to collect an invoice for a purchase, then to pay the invoice, and then to pick up the books. Why? Because Christina, who was snotty about the 'lower orders', didn't trust her sales staff to handle cash. Meanwhile, shelves were organized by publisher, rather than author or topic. The shop acquired such a reputation for confusion, in fact, that Dillons book chain ran an advert on a bus shelter on Charing Cross Road: *'Foyled again?'* it read. *'Try Dillons.'*

Foyles had the last laugh, however. Dillons disappeared in the 1990s. Foyles remains on Charing Cross Road – albeit in a new, even bigger headquarters.

G ot a spare few hours, a generous expense account and a desire to drink enough to fell an elephant? Well then, you might want to take inspiration from these famous publishing watering holes.

1. RULES RESTAURANT
(34–35 Maiden Lane, WC2E)

Open since 1798, Rules has hosted numerous publishers and their clients, John Murray and Byron among them – and is also the restaurant where Max Reinhardt and Anthony Blond scrawled an agreement on the back of a menu for the publication of Graham Greene's *The Tenth Man*: 'The Tenth Man to be published by BH [Bodley Head] and AB [Anthony Blond] . . . giving GG a larger royalty and the lion's share of foreign rights.' Greene was also very fond of Rules himself: it's one of the key meeting places in *The End of the Affair*, with adultery committed over the steak and pork chops.

2. THE YORK MINSTER (now the French House)
(49 Dean Street, W1D)

Once the York Minster, this drinking and eating hole became known as the French House in the 1940s when Charles de Gaulle formed the Free French Forces there. Now, a French flag is flown outside. Known for serving only half-pints ('more French'), its customers have included Wyndham Lewis, Aleister Crowley, Auberon Waugh (1939–2001) and Anthony Burgess. It was also here in February 1960 that Sylvia Plath signed up to publish *The Colossus* with Heinemann.

In spite of the liberation of the 1960s – and in spite of wonderful female editors like Diana Athill (1917–2019) at André Deutsch – publishing houses were still largely being run by men. A fact that provided for an animated conversation in a Goodge Street pub in 1972, where Carmen Callil (1938–2022) was having a drink, on a lunch break from her publicity work for the first issue of the feminist magazine *Spare Rib*. It was a light-bulb moment. She got together with some like-

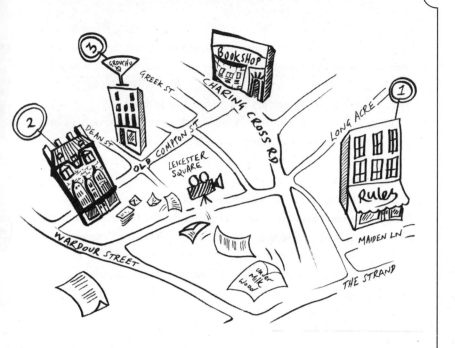

3. THE GROUCHO CLUB

(45 Dean Street, W1D)

This famous/infamous watering hole was set up by the publishers Carmen Callil and Liz Calder along with agent Ed Victor (1939–2017). They took its name from Groucho Marx, who famously quipped that he'd never join a club that would have him as a member.

minded friends, and – after initially settling on Spare Rib Books – they came across the name Virago (a woman who fights) in a dictionary about goddesses. Their logo, a bitten apple, was drawn by the cover designer of *The Female Eunuch*, and in 1975 they began operations from Callil's house in Cheyne Row, Chelsea, before moving in 1977 to the fourth floor of 5 Wardour Street, Soho, above a pinball arcade and a gentleman's hairdresser. From there, they published classic after classic, and proved that 'the other 50 per cent' of the population were just as interested in books as men – and just as able to publish them. In spite of their success, and undoubted brilliance, life in the Sisterhood wasn't always cosy. There was even a rumour that no one liked going to the toilet because there was generally a member of staff in there, sobbing.

Eventually, Virago went the way of most indies and was bought by a larger conglomerate, but dozens have sprung up since. At the time of writing, London is home to Influx Press (operating from Tottenham, and enjoying cheap rents thanks to the presence of a huge waste-management site next to their offices), Peirene Press in Holloway, Fitzcarraldo Editions in Knightsbridge, and CB Editions in poet-owner Charles Boyle's house, off the Uxbridge Road. There are dozens more mid-sized houses, and the big five British publishers Penguin Random House, Macmillan, HarperCollins, Hachette and Simon & Schuster are all still in the capital, publishing and encouraging many of the finest writers in the world.

KEY ADDRESSES
50 Albemarle Street, W1S (Tube station: Piccadilly Circus, Green Park)
8 Vigo Street, W1S (Tube station: Piccadilly Circus, Green Park)
Hogarth House, 32–34 Paradise Road, TW9 (Tube station: Richmond)
Cecil Court, WC2 (Tube station: Tottenham Court Road)
Hatchards, 187 Piccadilly, W1J (Tube station: Piccadilly Circus, Green Park)

RECOMMENDED READING
Diana Athill, *Stet*
Helene Hanff, *84 Charing Cross Road*
Mick Farren, *Give the Anarchist a Cigarette*
Fay Weldon, *Big Women*

CHAPTER SIXTEEN
ANGRY YOUNG MEN . . .

—ᗰᗰ—

I n the 1950s London was still a bombed-out mess. Swathes of streets were in ruins and progress on reconstruction was slow and piece-meal. There was rationing. And there was no good coffee. But there was also change in the air. There was a burgeoning youth culture, with skiffle clubs opening up all over Soho, Teddy Boys running amok in the suburbs, and *The Goon Show* bringing a new brand of uproarious surrealism to the BBC.

Also converging on the capital were a group of middle- and work-ing-class writers from industrial towns and rural backwaters, frustrat-ed with the status quo and determined to excoriate the establishment. John Osborne (1929–94) blew in from what he called the 'cultural desert' of Surrey, having also done time at boarding school, Stoneleigh, in Devon – from which he was expelled after whacking the headmaster (who had hit him for listening to a broadcast of Frank Sinatra). Colin Wilson arrived precociously young and fresh from Leicester and his job in a wool factory. John Braine (1922–86) descended from Bingley, near Bradford. Alan Sillitoe (1928–2010) came down from Notting-ham. Kingsley Amis (1922–95) – in actual fact a Londoner (raised in Norbury) – returned from exile at Oxford University, alongside Philip Larkin from Coventry (1922–85). Harold Pinter (1930–2008) was a Londoner too, but from the working-class 'suburbs' (Hackney, where his father worked as a tailor).

In the late 1950s, they became known as the Angry Young Men, although none of them much liked the term. Even the publisher Tom Maschler, who edited *Declaration*, a collection of political–literary essays by the 'Angries', said: 'They do *not* belong to a united movement. Far from it; they attack one another directly or indirectly in these pages. Some were even reluctant to appear between the same covers with others whose views they violently oppose.'

> **'To be shockingly original in your first novel, you don't have to discover a new technique: Simply write about people as they are and not as the literary establishment believes they ought to be.'**
>
> John Braine

But the label stuck, and has been understood ever since to apply to these young (white) male writers, who were so dissatisfied with traditional British society – and so determined to express their annoyance.

In spite of the writers' opposition to being Angry Young Men, the phrase also provided useful publicity. In fact, it's thought that the term was first coined at the Royal Court Theatre in 1956 to promote the John Osborne play *Look Back in Anger*. This play was set in a dingy flat in the Midlands – and the audience, used to more rarified stage sets, were shocked by the sight of the unkempt room (which included – *horror!* – an ironing board). BBC Radio called it 'unspeakably dirty and squalid', wondering how the male lead's wife could have such low standards; the *Daily Mail* lamented that such a pretty actress would be degraded by having to spend her time on stage ironing: 'She seems to have taken on the nation's laundry.' In contrast, Alan Sillitoe noted approvingly: 'Osborne doesn't contribute to British theatre, he sets off a landmine and blows most of it up.'

There's nothing like notoriety. After a twenty-minute documentary on TV, the play took off. Michael Halifax, the stage director at the Royal Court, said: 'After the TV extract, all these people started arriving. People you never see in theatres. Young people gazing around and wondering where to go and what the rules were.'

The play crystallized the idea that something was taking place. People started to say that *Lucky Jim*, Kingsley Amis's comic masterpiece (from back in 1954), reflected the same frustrations. John Braine's *Room at the Top* was an even bigger hit in 1957, and again showed a young man struggling against his origins – and those who held his origins against him. Arthur Seaton's rage at his mundane job is equally clear in Alan Sillitoe's *Saturday Night and Sunday Morning*, which followed in 1958. In the same year Arnold Wesker (1932–2016) brought political heat in *Chicken Soup with Barley*. They might not all have been saying precisely the same thing – but to outsiders at least, these men shared the same fiery spirit.

'If you can't annoy somebody, there is little point in writing.'

Kingsley Amis

The launch of *Declaration* in 1957 was another furious affair. It was originally supposed to be held at the Royal Court – but the management banned it, objecting to John Osborne's republican views. The party was held instead at the Pheasantry at 152–154 King's Road in Chelsea (then a private club with peerless bohemian credentials, now a Pizza Express). As well as the numerous authors, the launch attracted politicians, publishers and a whole heap of zeitgeist-chasing upper classes – who turned out to be unused to the kind of social levelling on display. Doris Lessing (1919-2013) later recalled the raucous gathering falling silent when the cut-glass voice of an aristocratic young woman rang out, demanding to know: 'Who *are* all these furry little people?'

'When I wrote my first two plays, The Kitchen **and** Chicken Soup with Barley**, I imagined I was traditionally recreating experience. But no, I was told, I was being an angry young man. A what? Me? Angry? Hadn't I been saying I couldn't write unless I was happy?'**

Arnold Wesker

After serving time as a radical in the 1950s, Kingsley Amis grew into an even angrier old man, ending his days holding forth in the Garrick Club and living in bourgeois splendour on Regent's Park Road in Primrose Hill – catching a taxi between his house and the pub when he could no longer manage the walk. His opinions became decidedly right-wing, and he even went to lunch with Margaret Thatcher. But he still wrote fine books like *The Old Devils*.

His son Martin Amis (1949–2023) also managed a reasonable amount of angry young literature himself, with books like *Money* (featuring the quintessential London hedonist John Self) and *London Fields* sending up the 1980s capital with stinging vitriol.

One of the less comfortable fits with the movement – or any movement, come to that – was Colin Wilson, who in 1956 released *The Outsider*, an overview of the concept of alienation in fiction (as well as the necessity of it). The book received rave reviews and sold by the bucketload – luckily for Wilson, who until that time had been living in dire poverty. When he'd first moved to London in 1953, he had decided to save on rent by buying a tent and sleeping on Hampstead Heath. He would spend his days writing in the British Museum reading room, before heading back to Hampstead. Barry Miles (again in *London Calling*) says that when Wilson told his writer friend Bill Hopkins about this routine, Hopkins responded: 'That's the idea, Col. Build up the legend!' But it was all too true. Wilson eventually ran out of money and took a job at the Lyon's Corner House on Coventry Street – and carried on sleeping outdoors. By the time *The Outsider* was published, he was at least living with his girlfriend Joy at 24 Chepstow Villas in Notting Hill – although subsisting on sausages, beer and chocolate biscuits. After the first edition of *The Outsider* sold out in two days, reporters began to queue up at his door. Wilson liked to invite them up and tell them that he was the 'next Plato'.

Although the Angry Young Men declined association and professed not even to like each other that much, quite a few of them did tend to hang out in the same places. The poet Dom Moraes (1938–2004) said that 'every young writer in town' used David Archer's bookshop on 34 Greek Street. Archer (1907–71) was a rich man who didn't care about making money (in fact, he sold cakes at a loss in the shop coffee bar, and gave coffee free to many regulars). He really just wanted to run a literary salon – and often discouraged people from buying his books, directing them instead to Foyles around the corner. (He is even said to have sent away people eager to buy *The Outsider*, when Colin Wilson was sitting in the shop, willing to sign copies.)

Aside from Archer's shop, the young writers also used to head for cheap coffee to the French Café on Old Compton Street – where, according to Quentin Crisp (1908–99), 'cosy, friendly, poverty-stricken writers, ill-equipped to live' would sit nursing empty mugs (one drink an hour was the rent).

In 1959, tiring of the fame that *Look Back in Anger* had brought him (though he didn't tire of the money, which paid for a huge house in Chelsea), John Osborne wrote a musical about gossip columnists called *The World of Paul Slickey*. The play received vitriolic reviews, and after the first night Osborne was chased up Charing Cross Road by a mob of furious theatregoers.

The new generation also congregated at the Colony Room, a private club owned by Muriel Belcher (1908–79), who was fond of calling her numerous patrons 'cunt' (if she were abusing them) or 'cunty' (if she meant to be affectionate). Muriel had a starring role as 'Mabel' in one of the last great works of the Angry Young Men – and one of the few actually set in London – Colin MacInnes's 1958 novel, *Absolute Beginners*.

'I love this city,' declares the protagonist on a taxi ride down the Embankment, and the novel, forming a picaresque journey through

Soho, central and west London, charts the newly formed youth culture, its fixation on jazz, clothes and coffee bars, associations with down-and-outs, bohemian easy sexuality and saying shocking things. It was a huge influence on the burgeoning mod culture – and one of the great signposts on the way to the next youth rebellion in the Swinging London of the 1960s.

KEY ADDRESSES

The Pheasantry, 152–154 King's Road, SW3 (Tube station: Sloane Square)
Royal Court Theatre, Sloane Square, SW1W (Tube station: Sloane Square)
24 Chepstow Villas, W11 (Tube station: Ladbroke Grove)
The Colony Room (now closed), 41 Dean Street W1D (Tube station: Tottenham Court Road)

RECOMMENDED READING

Kenneth Allsop, *The Angry Decade*
Kingsley Amis, *Lucky Jim*
John Braine, *Room at the Top*
Colin MacInnes, *Absolute Beginners*
Barry Miles, *London Calling*
John Osborne, *Look Back in Anger*
Colin Wilson, *The Outsider*

CHAPTER SEVENTEEN
. . . AND WOMEN

—⟋⟍—

For long centuries literary women in London were sidelined, ignored and even forbidden to write. In *A Room of One's Own* Virginia Woolf said that in early modern Britain a woman with 'brains and character' could not be heard. 'She never writes her own life and scarcely keeps a diary; there are only a handful of her letters in existence. She left no plays or poems by which we can judge her.'

Woolf wasn't entirely correct – women were writing, and there are a few literary remains, even from the seventeenth century and earlier. But the fact that they are so little-known speaks volumes – or rather, says something about that distinct lack of volumes. So too does the fact that women were banned from the stage in Shakespeare's era, or that even as late as the nineteenth century, many superb female artists felt unable to publish under their own names. It wasn't for fun that Mary Ann Evans called herself George Eliot, or that the Brontë sisters decided to first appear as the Bell brothers.

Yet in spite of all the odds, plenty of rebellious female voices did make themselves heard throughout the history of literary London from Margery Kempe onwards (and before, if you include Tacitus's account of Boudicca).

Even when women were banned from the stage, and made to stand primarily as muse and inspiration to the work of men, the voice of dissent broke through. Shakespeare himself wrote characters like Beatrice in *Much Ado About Nothing*, who threatens to dress the hero in her 'apparel and make him my waiting gentlewoman'. And in *A Midsummer Night's Dream* there's of course Titania, who jump-starts the action by refusing to submit to Oberon. Lady Macbeth and Cleopatra aren't to be messed with, either.

Meanwhile, off-stage, the real-life Londoner Mary Frith (1584–1659) was starting out in her career in the Fleet Street underworld. Wearing trousers, smoking a pipe and saying what the hell she liked, Frith inspired at least two plays: *The Mad Pranckes of Mery Moll of the Bankside* by John Day (*c.*1574–*c.*1638) and *The Roaring Girl* by Thomas Middleton (1580–1627) and Thomas Dekker (*c.*1572–1632). She also liked to tread the boards herself. In 1611 she entertained the audience at the Fortune Theatre, singing songs, heckling, and playing the lute. Despite numerous punishments – including time in the stocks – for her male dress and outspoken manner, she remained unrepentant, and continued to wear trousers until her death in 1659.

By this time, Aphra Behn (*c.*1640–89) was also making her way to London. Soon she would be managing the Dorset Garden Theatre, in Dorset Street near Spitalfields, embarking on a career as a spy for Charles II and writing plays like *The Rover* and *Love Letters Between a Nobleman and His Sister*. In *A Room of One's Own* again, Virginia Woolf suggests that 'All women' should shower flowers over Behn's grave, because she has 'earned them the right to speak their minds'. (Should you wish to do so, Behn is buried in the East Cloister of Westminster Abbey.)

Twenty-six years after Aphra Behn was born there came Mary Astell (1666–1731), who lived in Chelsea, surrounded herself with a group of literary and outspoken women, and wrote books such as *A Serious Proposal to the Ladies*. 'If all men are born free,' she asked, 'how is it that all women are born slaves?' (No one knows where exactly in Chelsea she lived, but the fact that Astell Street in the area is named after her displays her enduring effect.)

In 1689, the year Behn died, Lady Mary Montagu was born. A woman of letters and editor of a political periodical, Montagu repeatedly challenged contemporary attitudes towards women. She also shone at the London Court, entertained the likes of Alexander Pope with her wit, and wrote a series of brilliant letters relating to her travels in Turkey, where her husband was ambassador. On her return, she introduced the smallpox inoculation to the UK. (To prove that it worked, the inoculation was offered to seven prisoners at Newgate Prison, instead of execution.)

Pope and Montagu later fell out. From *The Dunciad* onwards, most of his publications include an allegation against her, but her good name only grew, especially when *Embassy Letters from Turkey* was published following her death in 1762.

The Montagu name also lived on in the form of Elizabeth Montagu (1718–1800). Elizabeth wasn't actually related to Mary. She was born Elizabeth Scott, and took her surname through marriage to Edward Montagu (who *was* related to Lady Mary's husband). Yet although the same blood might not have run in the women's veins, a similar fire did. Elizabeth was one of the leading lights in the eighteenth-century 'Blue Stocking' movement, and was dubbed by Dr Johnson 'The Queen of the Blues'. She was also described as 'brilliant in diamonds, solid in judgement, critical in talk'.

The Blue Stocking Society was an informal set-up, which came into being when a group of privileged friends began to meet in the London home of Elizabeth Montagu (at Portman Square) as well as the abodes of other society hostesses, including Elizabeth Vesey (1715–91) and Frances Boscawen (1719–1805). Rebelling against the ingrained idea that women should in their spare time knit, sew, and leave the thinking to the men, guests were instead invited to talk on intellectual topics and exchange witty conversation. As James Boswell mansplained, 'It was much the fashion for several ladies to have evening assemblies, where the fair sex might participate in conversation with literary and ingenious men, animated by a desire to please. These societies were denominated Bluestocking Clubs.'

As to the 'bluestocking' moniker, it actually came about after the botanist Benjamin Stillingfleet (1702–71) turned up at one of their soirées absent-mindedly wearing blue woollen stockings. These were working man's tights, when the salon dress-code required white silk, but the blunder tickled the hostesses, who afterwards adopted the title to signify a certain rising above worldly vanity, and focus on the finer things (i.e., the life of the mind).

Despite the dowdy image of their titular garment, in their day the bluestockings were very glamorous. Their parties were glittering affairs held in lavishly decorated rooms and open only to the in-crowd.

Elsewhere, some of the most effective female revolutionaries did their shouting from the sidelines. Such a woman was Mary Wollstonecraft – the outsider's outsider.

Mary was actually born into relative comfort – in 1759, in Primrose Street, long since demolished, near modern-day Liverpool Street. Mary's grandfather lived in one of the grand Georgian houses on Fournier Street, after he amassed a small fortune as a silk weaver. But despite his money, he lived in an area for workers, dissenters and radical preachers. Liverpool Street and the environs of Spitalfields were full of tanneries, smelling strongly of the huge vats of urine used by them to help remove the hair from the hides. Any wealth was that of self-made men, and the locals entertained grave suspicions about the 'upper' classes. It was also a furiously proud community, and if anyone was foolish enough to walk down the street wearing French silk (as opposed to proper English fabric), they would find the clothes torn off their backs. A fine atmosphere then, for a future radical.

As happened to several other notable London writers, Mary's childhood was disrupted by her father's debts – which caused her to leave London aged five. She came back at fifteen, this time to Hoxton, at that point a slum and boasting three of London's most notorious asylums. She later recollected that seeing mentally ill people in the street was worse than seeing people starving to death: they were 'the most terrific of ruins – that of the human soul'. (She went on to set her final novel, *Maria*, in an asylum.) There was also, again, a thriving radical community, and the Hoxton Academy – now part of New College London – was founded there. It promoted revolution and taught the subversive idea that human beings were naturally good and deserved to be free (the opposite teaching from the Church of England's at the time).

It was also in Hoxton that a scholarly neighbour introduced Mary to the writings of the forward-thinking philosopher John Locke (1632–1704), and that she first encountered Locke's notion that a husband 'should have no more power' over his wife than 'she has over his life'. This was quite a statement in an age when it was legal to hit your wife, to imprison her if she tried to leave you, and when children were the legal property of the husband.

But Mary is most closely associated with Stoke Newington, where in 1784 she opened a freethinking school for girls along with her friend Fanny Blood (c.1759–86) and launched her radical writing career with the publication of a pamphlet: *Thoughts on the Education of Daughters*. She also attended the Green's radical Unitarian Church and made friends in the local cafés with political firebrands such as Benjamin Franklin (1706–90), Thomas Paine (1737–1809) and Joseph Priestley (1733–1804).

In early adulthood she lived in St Paul's Churchyard for a time, with her publisher and supporter Joseph Johnson (1738–1809). In 1787 she moved across the river to a house on George Street, Southwark, where she made a start on a novel, took in translation work, and contributed articles to Johnson's new radical journal, *Analytical Review*. In 1791 she moved again, this time heading north to Store Street, off Tottenham Court Road. It was while she was living there, and as a dinner guest at Johnson's with Thomas Paine, that she met William Godwin (though they didn't form a romantic link for a number of years).

'Taught from infancy that beauty is woman's sceptre, the mind shapes itself to the body, and roaming round its gilt cage, only seeks to adorn its prison.'

Mary Wollstonecraft

Mary was also at Store Street when she published *A Vindication of the Rights of Woman* in 1792, advocating equality of the sexes and attacking men for encouraging excessive emotion in women. This cheeky riff on

Paine's great work *A Vindication of the Rights of Man*, written by a single, financially independent mother, caused equal acclaim and revulsion. But Mary wasn't content just to talk about change. She soon made off to revolutionary France, where she met Gilbert Imlay, became his lover, had his baby – and was then abandoned by him, prompting her suicide attempt at Putney Bridge (see p. 29).

After recovering she moved to Cumming Street, Pentonville, and sought solace with her neighbour William Godwin. She stayed with him until her death, in 1797, of puerperal fever, ten days after giving birth to her soon-to-be famous daughter Mary Shelley.

In common with most of the other places Wollstonecraft lived, the Cumming Street house no longer survives. If you want to pay homage to her, you need to head to her grave site in St Pancras Churchyard. And if you do, you'll be following in the footsteps of Mary Shelley. The first words she learned to read were those in the epitaph on her mother's grave: 'Mary Wollstonecraft Godwin – Author of the Vindication of the Rights of Women'. It was here too that Mary the younger (aged just seventeen) first arranged secret trysts with (the married) Percy Shelley, and declared her love for him. (Mary Wollstonecraft's body, along with her daughter's, has since been moved to a churchyard in Bournemouth, but there is still a memorial in St Pancras.)

Mary proved herself her mother's daughter, pressing against the restrictive conventions of her society. After eloping, she and Percy Shelley lived in Marchmont Street, in an unconventional trio with Mary's teenage stepsister Claire Clairmont (1798–1879).

Claire Clairmont is thought to be the subject of Shelley's poem 'To Constantia, Singing'. She also had an affair and a child with Byron, a frequent visitor – before he unceremoniously took the child and dumped Claire. There's a further rumour that she had another child with Shelley.

At the house on Marchmont Street, the Shelleys, Clairmont and Byron talked up the notions of free living and free love, but according to the only recently discovered memoirs of Claire Clairmont (found in 2009), it wasn't all sweetness and light. Byron and Shelley, she wrote in her later years, 'were monsters of lying, meanness, cruelty and treachery', 'worshippers of free love' who 'preyed on one another'. Possibly the bitter words of an old lady, but on the other hand, a good indication of how women stood to be abused, even by left-leaning radicals professing gender equality.

Mary Shelley took her share of hardship too. After her husband's death in Europe in 1822, she stayed on the Continent for a year, determined to earn a living through her pen, but was forced back to London in 1823. She lived first with her father and stepmother on the Strand and then in various places, on a tiny allowance from her incredibly wealthy father-in-law, Sir Timothy Shelley, which kept her and her son alive, but in poverty. The money was also only forthcoming on the proviso that Mary did not write any kind of memoir or recollections of her husband – although she did continue to write a series of fine novels following her horror classic *Frankenstein*. Several of them (in a manner that would have made her mother proud) argued both for better political systems and for humans to treat each other more fairly. Clearly, her father-in-law took little notice – although in 1846, on the death of the stingy Sir Timothy, Mary's son came into his inheritance and she lived in an improved degree of comfort at 24 Chester Square, Knightsbridge, until she died there of a suspected brain tumour in 1851.

By then, *Jane Eyre* had been published, and Becky Sharp had declared, 'I have brains,' in Thackeray's *Vanity Fair* (also that 'almost all the rest of the world are fools'). Soon there came geniuses like George Eliot. And firebrands like Annie Besant (1847–1933), the writer and social activist credited with the unrest and rallies of the unemployed that led to Bloody Sunday in Trafalgar Square in 1887; she was also one of the organizers of the London matchgirls' strike of 1888.

By the 1850s women had started to organize. No. 19 Langham Place in London became the office of the *English Woman's Journal* in

1858, boasting a reading room, coffee shop and meeting space, and very consciously promoted itself as a counterpoint to the gentleman's clubs endemic in the city. In its open discussion and support of employment issues and equality, it also helped launch a new wave of feminism and, ultimately, the suffragette movement.

The idea of female suffrage was already in the air in 1865, when John Stuart Mill introduced the idea when standing for parliament. The idea continued to grow, and numerous suffrage societies had been founded by the end of the nineteenth century. Among them was the Women's Franchise League, founded in 1889 by Emmeline Pankhurst (1858–1928) in her house at 8 Russell Square, which became an early hub for the movement (as was later recounted in her autobiography *My Own Story*).

> **'On Friday, 8th October 1909, Christabel Pankhurst and I were on our way to Newcastle. I had made up my mind that I was going to throw a stone. We went to the Haymarket [Central London] where the car with Mr Lloyd George would probably pass. As the motor appeared I stepped out into the road, stood straight in front of the car, shouted out, "How can you, who say you back the women's cause, stay on in a government which refuses them the vote, and is persecuting them for asking it," and threw a stone at the car. I aimed low to avoid injuring the chauffeur or passengers.'**
>
> Constance Lytton, *Prisons and Prisoners*

By the turn of the twentieth century, the suffragettes were in full flow – and busy chaining themselves to Buckingham Palace, setting fire to Mayfair post boxes, smashing Westminster windows, slashing paintings in the National Gallery – and very occasionally detonating bombs. They were also clogging up the London prison system. Over a thousand were incarcerated before the First World War, and contrary to the image of the jolly suffragette (perpetuated by such films as *Mary*

Poppins), these women were actually treated abysmally. Many were force-fed, leaving them with health issues for years. Constance Lytton (1869–1923), the upper-class suffragette and author of the memoir *Prisons and Prisoners*, endured such cruel treatment in London's Holloway Prison that her health never recovered.

As well as inspiring a multitude of memoirs, the suffragette movement developed its own genre of 'suffrage novels', aimed at furthering the cause – like *Suffragette Sally*, by Gertrude Colmore (1855–1926), published in London in 1911.

Constance Maud (1857–1929) published *No Surrender* in the same year, with a final sentence stating: 'the hour of dawn was nearing ... the claims of women would never more be pushed aside'. Alas, she had to wait another seventeen years for full suffrage to come about. Meanwhile, in 1918 Marie Stopes (1880–1958), a Fabian Society regular, published *Married Love*, espousing gender equality in marriage and the importance of female sexual desire. Ten years later, Virginia Woolf published the classic plea for female recognition, *A Room of One's Own* (followed by *Three Guineas* after another ten years, in 1938).

By this time, the career of another famous and brilliant suffragette author, Rebecca West (1892–1983), was also in full flow. West was born in Brixton, growing up in 21 Streatham Place, which she later depicted as 21 Lovegrove Place in *The Fountain Overflows*. (Sadly, the house has since been demolished and replaced by a fast-food restaurant.)

Rebecca West's birth name was Cicely Fairfield. She changed it in 1911, after she started writing for London's *Freewoman* magazine (partly to assuage her mother, who was worried about her outspoken views) – and took 'Rebecca West' from the Henrik Ibsen play *Rosmersholm*. In *Rosmersholm*, Rebecca West is the mistress of a married man who persuades her lover to join her in a melodramatic suicide by drowning.

West got her first break as a journalist after the success of a letter she had published in the *Scotsman*, at the age of fifteen. This was headed 'Women's Electoral Claims' and castigated the Liberal Party for its refusal to acknowledge the 'profound national effects of the subjection of women'. Soon she was writing for radical London magazines like *Clarion* and the *Freewoman*.

It was in the *Freewoman* that she described H. G. Wells as 'the Old Maid among novelists' in a crushing 1912 article. Wells invited her to dinner after reading it – and must have won West around. They became lovers (at the time, Wells was forty-six, West just twenty), and continued a passionate affair until, a year later, West found herself pregnant and packed off to a life of 'hateful domesticity' in Tunbridge Wells. Fortunately this was temporary, and West ploughed on, writing novels and criticism, refusing to bow to public approbation. In 1916, she put out a book landing several hard smacks on the recently deceased Henry James, his attitude to women and his overblown sentences. The following year, her novel *The Return of the Soldier* was published to wide acclaim – including from West herself: 'I suppose I ought not to say it is good,' she wrote, 'but it is.'

'I had never met anything like her before, and I doubt there was anything like her before.'

H. G. Wells on Rebecca West

West also took on D. H. Lawrence in a substantial critical work published in 1930 (when she was living at 15 Orchard Court, near Portman Square) and continued to write until deep into the second half of the twentieth century, reporting unflinchingly on the rise of Nazism in Yugoslavia, the Nuremberg trials, and the problems of communism and McCarthyism in the 1950s.

Also concerned with communism in the 1950s was Nobel Prize-winner Doris Lessing (1919–2013). After moving to the UK from South Africa in 1949, Lessing helped kick-start second-wave feminism with her novel *The Golden Notebook*, in 1962. The novel examined the Communist Party in England from the 1930s to the 1950s and also took on the budding women's liberation movement. 'Women are the cowards they are,' she wrote, 'because they have been semi-slaves for so long.'

Soon after arriving in London, Lessing paid a visit to 16 King Street in Covent Garden. This was the headquarters of the British Communist Party for most of the twentieth century – although by the 1950s the Party was in decline. When Doris Lessing turned up in 1952, she was asked why she was joining when so many other intellectuals were jumping ship. The official said that he looked forward to reading her future denunciations of communism – which she duly offered in a bitter magazine article in 1956, following the brutal suppression of the Hungarian uprising. She also, true to his predictions, resigned. Nevertheless, MI5 were convinced she was a spy for Russia, amassing one of the biggest surveillance files they have, and going to the extremes of tailing her on flights and breaking into her flat. 'An attractive, forceful, dangerous woman' was how they described her, with an apartment that was a hotbed of 'immoral activities'.

By the late 1950s, plenty of other female writers had started to take on the patriarchal status quo. Lynne Reid Banks (1929–), for example, wrote about run-down London boarding houses and single motherhood in *The L-Shaped Room* (1960). Single motherhood appeared again (in a not-quite-swinging London) in *The Millstone* (1965) by Margaret Drabble (1939–). And in the late 1960s, when she wasn't working as a sex therapist for the London underground magazine *Oz* or lighting up the King's Road (where she lived), Germaine Greer (1939–) was busily writing her 1970 masterpiece *The Female Eunuch*. According to Greer, the traditional nuclear family unit was one of the main issues when it came to gender equality, and women needed to stop accepting subservient domestic roles in the home (she also, somewhat provocatively, suggested her readers taste their own menstrual blood). Soon after the publication of *The Female Eunuch*, feminist activists disrupted the 1970 Miss World contest at the Royal Albert Hall. At the sound of a whistle, they threw stink bombs and flour bombs, fired water pistols and chanted, 'We are not beautiful, we are not ugly, we are angry.' The event was broadcast to 30 million people. The fight was on.

This period also saw a mushrooming of collective literary presses and magazines in London. *Spare Rib* hit the news stands. Virago Press stocked the bookshops with Storm Jameson (1891–1986) and Rebecca West. The Women's Press started in a tiny office off Goodge Street, from where it introduced the likes of Alice Walker (1944–) to the UK. There were also important bookshops: Silver Moon on Charing Cross Road (64–68), Sisterwrite in Islington (190 Upper Street) and, opening in 1975 and still (just about) going, The Feminist Library, currently at 5 Westminster Bridge Road.

By 1975, Angela Carter (1940–92) had also arrived back in London after spending two years in Tokyo. She'd been in Japan, after putting the proceeds of winning the Somerset Maugham award towards running away from her husband. While there, she said, she 'learnt what it is to be a woman and became radicalized'. She moved to south London's Tooting Bec and dedicated the following two decades to creating strong female Londoners: Fevvers in *Nights at the Circus* (a Cockney 'virgin' hatched from an egg and brought up in Ma Nelson's East End whorehouse); Dora and Nora Chance in *Wise Children*, with their sprawling theatrical family in Brixton; Melanie and her uncle's strange toyshop in Crystal Palace ... Tragically, Carter died aged just fifty-one, in 1992.

At least by 1992, Constance Maud's longed-for dawn had come. The fight continues – but no one will be able to deny women's place in London literary life again.

KEY ADDRESSES

East Cloister, Westminster Abbey, Dean's Yard, SW1P (Tube station: Westminster)

Montagu House, 22 Portman Square, W1H (Tube station: Marble Arch)

Hoxton Academy, N1 (Tube station: Old Street)

St Pancras Churchyard, NW1 (Tube station: Mornington Crescent)

24 Chester Square Mews, SW1W (Tube station: Victoria)

19 Langham Place, W1B (Tube station: Oxford Circus)

9 Russell Square (now part of the Russell Hotel), WC1N (Tube station: Russell Square)

RECOMMENDED READING

Germaine Greer, *The Female Eunuch*

Doris Lessing, *The Golden Notebook*

Emmeline Pankhurst, *My Own Story*

Mary Wollstonecraft, *A Vindication of the Rights of Woman*

Virginia Woolf, *A Room of One's Own; Three Guineas*

CHAPTER EIGHTEEN

BEATS AND HIPPIES

—⁓⁓—

n 1958, Kenneth Allsop (1920–73) wrote a survey of the previous ten years called *The Angry Decade*. In the final pages, he declared that it was time to simmer down. Rockets were on the way to the moon and anger was of limited use. It was time, he said for 'love'. It was also, as American theatre director Charles Marowitz (1934–2014) said, time to party. And everyone wanted to do it in London.

'London is the most swinging city in the world at the moment.'

Vogue, 1965

By the late 1960s, when women were buying miniskirts at Mary Quant's Bazaar on the King's Road and hairy men were picking up kaftans on Carnaby Street, over 40% of the UK population was under the age of twenty-five. In London, weekly earnings far out-stripped the average cost of living. It was a good time to be young – and youngsters set the agenda not just in literature but in music, dress and art. They even changed the language – the polyglot slang in Anthony Burgess's *A Clockwork Orange* was, in part, an extreme reflection of London's developing street language, as well as a riff on various Slavic, Russian and American influences.

It wasn't all counterculture. Hatchards wasn't ashamed to stock books like Harper Lee's *To Kill a Mockingbird*; Lampedusa's *The Leopard*; or endless copies of Agatha Christie. There was plenty of good stuff happening in the mainstream. But the decade has become best known for those hippies and Beats who followed the Angry Young Men of the 1950s into the coffee bars, bookshops and clubs of an ever more colourful capital.

Leading the first wave, as he so often did, was William Burroughs. He visited London for several short spells in the early 1960s, before finally settling at 22 Dalmeny Court, Duke Street, St James's. As often, he was looking for a heroin cure – but this was also a productive period. It was at the kitchen table in Dalmeny Court that he developed his influential cut-up technique. He also entertained himself by projecting risqué films from his window onto the walls of the nearby London Library at night.

When Burroughs wasn't busy furthering the avant-garde, he also liked to stroll around his upmarket neighbourhood – because although Burroughs was one of the leaders of the decidedly grungy new generation, he also had very particular tastes. On the advice of Antony Balch (1937–80), his lover and collaborator, he had his shoes hand-made at John Lobb, just around the corner on St James's Street (with customers from Duke Ellington to the Duke of Edinburgh), and also indulged in a wide-brim Montecristi panama hat from James Lock (again, on St James's). He shopped for his groceries at Fortnum and Mason ('tonight we are to have wild duck', he enthused in one of his letters home).

There were other pleasures to be found locally: Burroughs was partial, in particular, to the entrance of the Regent Palace Hotel, a favourite haunt of young male prostitutes. It was locally known as 'The Meat Rack' – and had been since the nineteenth century, when another customer had been Oscar Wilde.

It was also in London in November 1964 that the fiercely independent publisher John Calder published Burroughs's *The Naked Lunch* – and a legend was born. Before that, not all Burroughs's associations were so successful. On one of his earlier visits to London, in December 1960, he put on an action painting and poetry projection at the ICA, featuring manic dancing from the poet Brion Gysin (1916-86), a cut-up tape recording of Burroughs, Arab drumming and a light show by electronics wizard Ian Sommerville (1940-76). Half the audience left.

Burroughs disliked the Moka Bar on Frith Street in Soho. This was one of the first places cappuccino coffee was made available in London, but he didn't approve of their overly sweet offering. He also accused them of 'outrageous and unprovoked discourtesy and poisonous cheesecake' and started photographing the shop and making recordings inside, before playing them back outside on tape. This he believed, would create a 'new reality' and leave them 'seething'. He got his way when the Moka closed in 1972.

Another leading Beat, Allen Ginsberg, arrived in the capital in May 1965, drawn by letters from his friend Burroughs and wanting to get a proper look at just how 'swinging' London really was. Barry Miles, co-founder of Better Books (see p. 158), says that Ginsberg wasted no time on his arrival. He checked into his lodgings, offloaded his suitcases and found his way down Charing Cross Road to Miles's shop. There, together with Miles, Ginsberg arranged an impromptu free reading – for that very evening. This event, even though there wasn't time to advertise, was packed. Andy Warhol (1928–87) and Edie Sedgwick (1943–71) sat in the front row. Donovan (1946–) and his friend 'Gypsy' sat on the doorstep and offered a rendition of 'Cocaine Blues'. Jeff Nuttall, poet, general hipster-about-town, and counterculture icon, was also in attendance. He described the whole thing as like 'a healing wind on a very parched collective mind'. Far out. The night ended with Ginsberg naked, a pair of knickers on his head, and a 'Do not disturb' sign hanging around his nether regions.

But electrifying as the evening may have been, it was nothing compared with Ginsberg's next move. Realizing that Lawrence Ferlinghetti (1919–2021) and Gregory Corso (1930–2001) were also about to arrive in London, and buzzing from the success of the Better Books event, Ginsberg, the staff there, and some other key new-wave London literati decided to book the Albert Hall. They were going to have a proper 'happening' – and in one of the biggest and most respectable buildings in the capital.

The event took place on 11 June. Despite anxiety that they might end up with no more than an audience of 500 in the vast auditorium, over 7,000 people showed – and to an Albert Hall that had been transformed. The floor was strewn with flowers, caskets of wine and joints were passed around, and the psychiatrist R. D. Laing (1927–89) and a number of his schizophrenic patients added new meaning to the idea of audience participation by dancing wildly in the aisles.

R. D. Laing worked as a psychotherapist at the Tavistock Institute in London, and in 1967 opened his own clinic at Kingsley Hall near Bow, in the East End. He was a key player in the 1960s capital, writing best-selling books like *The Divided Self* (which presented mental illness as transformative and suggested that patients' feelings might be valid expressions of lived experience rather than delusions). Fans included Sylvia Plath (1932–63) and Ted Hughes (1930–98), and Laing was affectionately known about town as the 'Acid Marxist'. In the early Sixties, Sean Connery (1930–2020), stressed by filming James Bond, visited Laing at Kingsley Hall and asked for advice. Laing suggested LSD.

On the stage, Lawrence Ferlinghetti gave a mighty rendition of 'To Fuck Is to Love Again' and Allen Ginsberg was so drunk no one could understand him. But the performances were almost immaterial. It was an epochal moment in the cultural history of the 1960s. Many members of the audience later said that it wasn't just the poetry or the extravagant posturings of the performers – that the most galvanizing thing was looking around and realizing that they weren't the only freaks in town. There were thousands of them. The underground had risen.

WHERE TO JOIN THE HIGH SOCIETY

THE PARTISAN

In 1958, and partly financed by the writers John Berger (1926–2017) and Doris Lessing, the Partisan opened at 7 Carlisle Street, with the editorial offices of the *Left Review* journal above it. It boasted a hip, ultra-modern interior, provided a meeting place for the radical arts group Centre 42 – and was so eager to create a Parisian Left Bank atmosphere that it let most of its regulars drink for free. Unsurprisingly, it went bankrupt in 1962 – but not before Doris Lessing had written long tracts of her feminist classic, *The Golden Notebook*, at one of its tables.

THE ROUNDHOUSE

In 1964 the Roundhouse – a disused railway warehouse in north London's Chalk Farm – was appropriated by the playwright Arnold Wesker and his theatrical company Centre 42. The idea was to turn the building into a permanent cultural centre, complete with a theatre, art gallery, cinema and workshop space – and for the next decade it became the centre of the underground, hosting everything

KEY ADDRESSES

Burroughs's London address, 22 Dalmeny Court, Duke Street, SW1 (Tube station: Green Park)

Kingsley Hall, Powis Road, London, E3 (Tube station: Bromley-by-Bow)

The Royal Albert Hall, Kensington Gore, SW7 (Tube station: South Kensington)

The Roundhouse, Chalk Farm Road, NW1 (Tube station: Chalk Farm)

Site of Oz offices, 52 Princedale Road, W11 (Tube station: Holland Park)

from 'happenings' headlined by Pink Floyd to experimental theatre such as *Oh Calcutta!* by Kenneth Tynan (1927–1980), featuring an entirely nude cast. (When the play premiered, the Met sent two police officers to check out the show . . . one of them returned twice before deciding to press for obscenity charges.)

THE ARTS LAB

Founded in 1967 by new-wave guru Jim Haynes (1933–2021) and running for just two years, the Arts Lab – based at 182 Drury Lane – was nevertheless a hugely influential multidisciplinary arts centre dedicated to groovy 'happenings', including art exhibitions by John and Yoko, gigs by David Bowie (1947–2016), poetry readings and improvisational plays. 'When I went there last week,' wrote a *Guardian* journalist back in 1968, 'the place was crowded with classless youth, buying avant-garde magazines at the bookstall, sampling cheap and pleasantly experimental food in the cafeteria, and looking at two exhibitions of work by new painters.' There was also a play going on, with the actors 'squat[ting] in the centre of the theatre, where they free associate . . . One of them pointlessly smashes a cucumber.'

RECOMMENDED READING

Anthony Burgess, *A Clockwork Orange*
Quentin Crisp, *The Naked Civil Servant*
R. D. Laing, *The Divided Self*
Barry Miles, *London Calling: A Countercultural History of London Since 1945*
Jeff Nuttall, *Bomb Culture*

CHAPTER NINETEEN

SPIES AND COLD WARRIORS

—⚬—

The thing about the Secret Service is that it's . . . secret. Spying, literature and London have long gone hand in hand, but they have generally done so off the record and in the shadows. Espionage is a world of innuendo, whispered rumour and deceit – which is of course what makes it so fascinating, and such a good match for books and book people. No one can lie like a fiction writer, after all.

Early entanglements of literature and espionage came in Elizabethan London, as paranoid whispers about Catholic insurrection, Spanish invasion and Scottish plots swirled around murky Thames-side taverns and playhouses. Some even say that Shakespeare ran a government spy ring – although God alone knows how busy that would have made him. There are several more likely candidates. His fellow playwright Anthony Munday (*c.*1560–1633), for instance, who was appointed 'poet to the city' while Shakespeare was still writing, was also called 'our best plotter' by a contemporary, William Webbe (1568–91). Given how bad Munday's plays were, many people think that the plotting reference is really about his *other* activities: like the time he entered the English College in Rome under a false name, to check on the activities of exiled Catholics.

More famous than Munday is Christopher Marlowe (see p.13), the handsome, swashbuckling author of *The Jew of Malta* and *Dr Faustus*. Marlowe aroused suspicions because he kept disappearing to Europe and was once mysteriously arrested in the Netherlands, apparently for getting mixed up in a coin-counterfeiting operation, related to

Catholic sedition. He was just as mysteriously let go again – without charge. His death too has provoked much speculation. When he was killed in Deptford, on 30 May 1593, a contemporary author, Francis Meres (c.1565–1647), claimed he was 'stabbed to death by a bawdy serving-man, a rival of his in his lewd love' in a tavern brawl. But in fact, Marlowe was not in a pub but in a house. Its owner, Eleanor Bull (c.1550–96), had high-level government connections, and some also say that her home was a kind of safe house, and that the men with Marlowe were agents provocateurs. If he *was* spying on behalf of the Elizabethan Court, he got little thanks, since his body was chucked in an unmarked grave in St Nicholas churchyard, Deptford.

So much for the Elizabethans. London literary spies were even more active in the twentieth century.

Joseph Conrad, as he so often did, got there slightly before everyone else. If you buy one book on espionage, it has to be his 1907 novel *The Secret Agent*. This visionary masterpiece features a Russian-sponsored anarchist attempt to blow up the Greenwich Observatory. After reading Conrad's descriptions of sinister under-cover operations and pitiless folly, a walk in Greenwich Park will never be the same again.

G. K. Chesterton showed the continuing potential of the genre a year after Conrad, in *The Man Who Was Thursday* – again featuring a group of anarchists, and this time focusing on 'Gabriel Syme', a man who claims that the London Underground timetable is mankind's most poetical creation.

As the shadow of the First World War loomed darker, German undercover agents took over from anarchist upsetters. The classic First World War spy novel is *The Thirty-Nine Steps* by John Buchan (1875–1940), which starts with the hero Richard Hannay dining in the Café Royal in the West End and really gets going when a man named Scudder is murdered in Hannay's nearby flat ('on the first floor in a new block behind Langham Place' – a mere ten minutes' stroll north of Piccadilly, if you're feeling up to it: past Oxford Circus and just around the corner from the BBC). Meanwhile, Sir Arthur Conan

Doyle – similarly preoccupied with the conflagration across the Channel – also set Sherlock Holmes transmitting false information to Germany, and bringing a spy into Scotland Yard in *His Last Bow*.

Bolshevik revolutionaries became the main fear after the Russian Revolution in 1917. Arthur Ransome, the author of *Swallows and Amazons*, caused a scandal on his return to London in 1919 from communist Russia. When he arrived at King's Cross, he was arrested and taken for questioning by Special Branch, who suspected him of working for the enemy. When they asked him about his political affiliation, he said simply, 'Fishing'.

> **'I have a very fair turn of speed, and that night I had wings. In a jiffy I was in Pall Mall and had turned down towards St James's Park. I dodged the policeman at the Palace gates, dived through a press of carriages at the entrance to the Mall, and was making for the bridge before my pursuers had crossed the roadway. In the open ways of the Park I put on a spurt. Happily there were few people about and no one tried to stop me. I was staking all on getting to Queen Anne's Gate.'**
>
> John Buchan, *The Thirty-Nine Steps*

By the 1930s and into the Second World War the focus again fell on German infiltrators. Elizabeth Bowen (1899–1973) set *The Heat of the Day*, her novel of love, deception and double agents, among the London bombing raids. Her heroine finds herself trapped between a spy and counter-spy while living in Weymouth Street (near Harley Street and not far from Richard Hannay's flat) and the novel contains memorable descriptions of bombing raids. Bowen herself weathered the Blitz in a flat near Regent's Park. It was bombed in 1944, but luckily she wasn't hurt.

The Blitz also plays a big role in Graham Greene's *The Ministry of Fear*. When Arthur Lowe leaves his shabby Bloomsbury bedsit to go on the run, after unwittingly coming into possession of a much-coveted microfilm, it's onto the war-ravaged streets of the capital

EAT LIKE A SPY

SCOTT'S OF MAYFAIR

(20 Mount Street, London, W1K)

In *Diamonds Are Forever* (1956), Bond visits Scott's of Mayfair for 'dressed crab and a pint of Black Velvet' (a mix of sparkling wine and Guinness). Once, when Fleming was leaving the restaurant with a columnist on the *San Francisco Chronicle*, he said: 'See that window? When James Bond is in London, he always lunches there, at the corner table – that's so he can look down and watch the pretty girls walking past.'

WILTON'S

(55 Jermyn Street, London, SW1Y)

This old Jermyn Street restaurant – established in 1742 – is where, in Len Deighton's *The Ipcress File*, the secret service head Dalby treats a new recruit to a slap-up lunch. The gourmet narrator enjoys an 'iced Israeli melon, sweet, tender and cold like the blonde waitress'.

CAFÉ ROYAL

(68 Regent Street, London, W1B)

John Buchan doesn't mention the precise menu, but this is where Richard Hannay eats in *The Thirty-Nine Steps*, shortly before returning to his flat near Portland Place, discovering a dead body, and being plunged into a world of intrigue and deceit. Today you can still eat there, and despite recent refurbishment the Oscar Wilde Bar – previously the Grill Room – has been kept exactly as it was first decorated, in 1865.

– where he frequently finds himself contending with closed and cratered roads, Tube closures and smoking ruins, and having to make anxious calls to discover which parts of London have disappeared overnight. Bloomsbury and the environs spreading into Soho and Fitzrovia came naturally to Greene – and in the wartime he worked there: at the Ministry of Information, which was based in the Senate House at UCL.

Greene had become a spy. He was recruited to MI6 in 1941 by Kim Philby (1912–88), the infamous double agent and member of the 'Cambridge Five' whose betrayals would later inspire David Cornwell, aka John le Carré (1931–2020). Greene was chosen because of his access to high places, exotic locations, and general friendliness towards the champagne-swilling, left-leaning intelligentsia. He was asked to report on anyone who might be too well inclined towards the enemy. He didn't spot Philby though – and when he was exposed in 1963, Graham Greene was one of the few people to defend him. He argued that Philby's faith in communism was religious, and that religious faith trumps love of one's country. The two remained pen pals until Philby's death in 1988 – Philby writing from his apartment in Moscow; Greene from his villa in the south of France, where he was by then living. Despite this tricky relationship, Norman Sherry, Greene's biographer, has suggested that his subject continued to work for the British government until his death in 1991.

Ian Fleming (1908–64) also worked as a spy in the Second World War, although by the time he turned to writing in the 1950s, under the shadow of imminent nuclear annihilation, he focused on the Russians. His Cold War spy fiction was a glamorous affair. James Bond's fondness for smart clothes and luxury was inspired by Fleming's own lifestyle. Fleming had spent a good part of the 1930s enjoying the high life in a bachelor flat on Ebury Street, in Victoria, where he set up *Le cercle gastronomique et des jeux de hasard*: a private men-only dining club whose mission was to discover the perfect meal.

By the time he came to write about Bond, Fleming had set himself up in 16 Victoria Square, Westminster, his bedroom hung with green-striped Regency wallpaper and containing a small bust of Admiral Nelson. He loved old-fashioned splendour, but his attempts to create the perfect atmosphere were undermined by the post-war building going on around him. He particularly disliked the brutalist tower blocks popping up on his local skyline, built by one Ernö Goldfinger. Fleming got his revenge when he used the architect's name for his arch-villain and power-crazed weirdo, Auric Goldfinger.

The next great spy writer, John le Carré, like Buchan and Fleming before him, used many central London and West End locations. His characters live in Chelsea mews and hang out at gentlemen's clubs – the difference being that in Le Carré's world they're nearly all depressed and have to contend with near-perpetual rain. His is a London of darker shadows and deeper mysteries. We first catch sight of George Smiley, the hero of the classic *Tinker Tailor Soldier Spy* (1974), near Fleming's old house in Victoria, but in decidedly unglamorous circumstances. He is depicted 'scuttling' along the pavement near the 'blackened arcades' of the train station, rain misting his thick glasses. He lives on Bywater Street in Chelsea, which (while hardly the crime-filled streets of some parts of London) is portrayed as having houses with shuttered windows, kerbs packed with cars, and is clearly not a desirable locale. (Were Smiley around today, he'd surely be astonished at the current house prices ...)

Even when Smiley goes to Mayfair, it's to a melancholy casino off Grosvenor Square, with perpetually drawn curtains and 'meaningless' pictures of fruit in 'colossal gold frames'. Otherwise he moves through a dour and down-at-heel London: the 'meagre premises' of a chemist's shop on Charing Cross Road; half-ruined, bomb-damaged terraces in Camden; the Islay Hotel on Sussex Gardens – 'a fire-bowl of clashing wallpapers and copper lampshades' – where Smiley and his crew set up headquarters until they catch the mole in *Tinker Tailor Soldier Spy*. Even the headquarters for British Intelligence is located above a shabby shop at the traffic-choked corner of Shaftesbury Avenue and Charing Cross Road.

This crucial location, Le Carré told the *Daily Mail*, was based on a

REAL-LIFE SPY LOCATIONS

54 BROADWAY

(Tube station: St James's Park)

A sign on the front door said it was the office of a fire-extinguisher company, but in fact, until 1994 this building was the home of MI6. There was a secret entrance at the rear, at 21 Queen Anne Gate, through which the staff – including a young John le Carré – used to sneak.

MI6, 85 ALBERT EMBANKMENT

(Tube station: Vauxhall)

Nowadays MI6 is based at 85 Albert Embankment, a building rumoured to have five storeys of basements, to have been kitted out for 'bomb-blast resistance' (to the tune of £17 million), and to boast a secret tunnel to Whitehall.

296–302 BOROUGH HIGH STREET

(Tube station: London Bridge)

Until the 1990s, new recruits were sent to this unremarkable building in Borough High Street, where they would learn 'non-field techniques'. Yes, it was spy school.

35 PORTLAND PLACE

(Tube station: Regent's Park, Great Portland Street)

This innocuous Georgian house was once the location of a secret

building opposite Moss Bros on Cambridge Circus – 'which,' he said, 'had a lot of rather mysterious curved windows to it'. If you want further specifics, Le Carré fan and journalist-turned-sleuth Gordon Corera has suggested that the entrance described by Le Carré most closely resembles that of 90 Charing Cross Road, just north of the Circus itself. Those wanting to see the Circus as rendered in the 2011 laboratory that used real-life Qs to create outlandish gadgets – such as exploding rats.

HOLY TRINITY ORATORY, KNIGHTSBRIDGE
(Tube station: Knightsbridge)
Enter Holy Trinity Church through the right-hand door, and you'll see a small Pietà statue just to your right. To the left of this, behind two pillars, is a small place that KGB agents used for dead-letter drops, hiding cassette tapes and microfilms throughout the Cold War.

CAFÉ DAQUISE, KENSINGTON
(Tube station: South Kensington)
This Kensington landmark has been serving the same hearty Polish food since 1947, and it's also been the perennial favourite of a number of real-life spies, including 'Cambridge Five' members Kim Philby and Donald Maclean. Christine Keeler – star and victim of the Profumo affair – also had a soft spot for the restaurant, and frequently ate there with her KGB lover, Yevgeni Ivanov.

BOODLE'S, 28 ST JAMES'S STREET
(Tube station: Green Park)
One of the oldest members' clubs in London, and located at St James's Street since 1782, Boodle's has long been a favoured recruiting ground for MI6 officers, including James Bond author Ian Fleming. In the Bond novels the club is known as 'Blades' – M's watering-hole of choice.

Gary Oldman film should head for the disused Inglis Barracks in Mill Hill and Blythe House in Blythe Road near Kensington Olympia, whose grandly drab exteriors provided most of the shots.

While you're in Kensington, you might also head over to 50 Harrington Road, a crucial location in London spy literature. This is now an unprepossessing convenience store, but before the war it was the

Russian Tea Room, set up by the last naval attaché to the Imperial Russian Embassy in London, Admiral Nikolai Wolkoff. Wolkoff's daughter Anna was the secretary of the Right Club – a pro-Nazi organization, which met above the café. (She was also a dressmaker to the Nazi-favouring Wallis Simpson, better known as the Duchess of Windsor.) In 1939, Anna became friendly with a young code clerk at the US Embassy called Tyler Kent, who started passing her secret telegrams. But her spying career was ended when an MI5 agent named Joan Miller infiltrated the Right Club, gained Wolkoff's confidence and had her arrested at the Russian Tea Room under the Official Secrets Act.

This arrest was witnessed by an eleven-year-old boy whose mother worked at the café. His name was Leonard Cyril Deighton (1929–), and he grew up to write many successful spy novels, including *The Ipcress File*, which introduced the world to Harry Palmer and the gloriously bleak *Game, Set and Match* trilogy.

Deighton's vision of a war-battered and rundown city is possibly even grimier and sleazier than Le Carré's. In Deighton's London there are smutty screenings at secret cinemas on Charlotte Street, meetings in squalid Soho clubs (where little yellow bulbs wink 'lecherously' around signs advertising 'Non Stop Striptease Revues'). In *The Ipcress File*, Leicester Square is less the centre of the world than a place to buy dirty magazines.

'In London, where anything goes, just make sure it's not your wallet.'

Len Deighton

Don't worry if you'd rather not follow Deighton into this underworld: he does have a more palatable side. His food recommendations are superb. You can still, for example, buy coffee from the grandson of Mr Higgins, who sells beans to the bon vivant Dicky Cruyer in *London Match*. His shop is on Duke Street, near Grosvenor Square. You can also still visit Wilton's on Jermyn Street, which is mentioned in *The*

Ipcress File and has been doing good business since 1742. Sadly, you won't be able to call in at the Trattoria Terrazza, where the narrator of *The Ipcress File* heads to sink grappa. The building on Romilly Street in Soho is now occupied by a chain restaurant, but once it was renowned for its authentic Italian food (still quite a rarity in 1960s Britain). It was where Deighton wrote much of his first novel – 'comforted', he said, 'by bowls of fresh pasta' – and it was also where he met Michael Caine (1933–), planning his screen interpretation of Harry Palmer. 'It's difficult to believe now – but before the film came out, Michael was still a struggling actor and I was a famous writer,' Deighton told the *Independent* newspaper. 'Of course, he overtook me like a skyrocket, but there was a brief period of time when I was more famous than Michael.'

Fame is fickle. Deighton's books at least will last. Even if he was not (so far as we know, anyway) an actual spy, few writers have brought such realism to the genre, such palpable anger, or such style.

John le Carré notwithstanding, real spies are not always reckoned the best people to write about their craft. One of the best-known London spy writers from recent years is Stella Rimington (1935–). She worked in MI5 for three decades, starting out as a secretary and rising through the ranks to become Director-General, a position she held from 1992 to 1996. Her achievements in the field were considerable. She campaigned for greater openness about the service, and during her tenure, in 1993, published the MI5 booklet *The Secret Service*, which revealed publicly, for the first time, details of MI5's activities, operations and duties. Things went wrong after her retirement when she turned writer and, in 2001, published her memoirs, *Open Secret*. Sadly, these were widely decried as 'tedious' in the press. She has at least had better success with her spy novels. The first, *At Risk*, revolves around a British operative trying to foil a London-focused terrorist attack, and the *Guardian* conceded 'she is jolly good on magic mushrooms and the art of making bombs out of silly putty'.

KEY ADDRESSES

Greenwich Observatory, SE10 (Tube station: North Greenwich; rail: Greenwich)

16 Victoria Street, SW1 (Tube station: St James's Park)

Bywater Street, SW3 (Tube station: Sloane Square)

Sussex Gardens, W2 (Tube station: Paddington)

90 Charing Cross Road, W1D (Tube station: Tottenham Court Road)

50 Harrington Road, SW7 (Tube station: South Kensington)

RECOMMENDED READING

Elizabeth Bowen, *The Heat of the Day*

John Buchan, *The Thirty-Nine Steps*

G. K. Chesterton, *The Man Who Was Thursday*

Joseph Conrad, *The Secret Agent*

Len Deighton, *London Match*

Ian Fleming, *Casino Royale*; *Goldfinger*

Graham Greene, *The Ministry of Fear*

John le Carré, *Tinker Tailor Soldier Spy*; *The Spy Who Came In from the Cold*

CHAPTER TWENTY
IMMIGRANTS AND EXPATS

—◦◦◦—

M any ancient Athenians believed they were autochthonous – a race that sprang up direct from the soil of their city state. No such belief has ever been possible in London. It has always been a city to which outsiders have flocked, and has long been a melting pot of different races and creeds. Only a small proportion of the writers and characters in this book were actually born in London; even fewer have long-standing family connections with the city. London, really, is a city of immigrants, and has been for a very long time.

Chief among the capital's visitors have always been the French. Today it's often said that there are more French people in London than in Bordeaux, Nantes or Strasbourg. But our friends from across the Channel have been complaining about London's food at least since waves of Huguenots fleeing religious persecution landed there in the sixteenth century – and, arguably, since William the Conqueror set up base in London, following the Norman victory over King Harold in 1066.

In spite of this persistent moaning, one Frenchman at least arrived to make the most of things: Voltaire (1694–1778). The author of *Candide* breezed into town in 1726, declaring himself (oddly) delighted with the 'lovely' weather, and with having escaped the 'dungeon' of France (and more literally the Bastille, where he had recently been a prisoner). Voltaire lived in Wandsworth (exact address unknown), where he is said to have enjoyed arguing about water-baptism in Latin with Edward Higginson, a teacher at a local Quaker school. He also managed to learn to speak good English in three months, largely thanks to the time he spent at Drury Lane Theatre, watching Shakespeare plays and ogling the famous actress Anne Oldfield (1683–1730). He met Alexander Pope, John Gay and Jonathan Swift (1667–1745) – himself visiting from Ireland – not to mention a good portion of high society; but Voltaire's brief bright visit was cut short in 1728 when he left under a cloud, accused of embezzlement and doctoring cheques.

In 1765, Jean-Jacques Rousseau (1712–78) also came across the Channel, following the scandals provoked by the publication of *The Social Contract* and *Emile*. He initially lived at 10 Buckingham Street, just off the Strand, but hated the 'black vapours' there and soon moved out to Chiswick. Unfortunately, he didn't much like Chiswick, either, and moved away in 1766.

Ignatius Sancho, widely thought to be the first African writer in London, ran a grocery shop at 19 Charles Street (today King Charles Street) from 1773 until he died in 1780, selling tobacco, sugar and tea. He was a former slave, but had a classical education, wrote poetry and plays (not to mention music), was a friend of Dr Johnson and Laurence Sterne and had his portrait painted by Gainsborough. After his death his letters were published; they became a major best-seller.

Paul Verlaine (1844–96) had a more favourable view of London. He visited in September 1872 with his lover and fellow poet Arthur Rimbaud (1854–91), and called it 'the city of the Bible'. The pair set up house at 34 Howland Street in Fitzrovia, on what is now the site of the British Telecom Tower. Rimbaud also enjoyed London at first, particularly favouring the plentiful absinthe available in Soho and the facilities in the British Library, where the poverty-stricken poet noted approvingly that 'heating, lighting, pens and ink were free'. Sadly he and

Verlaine split up – over an argument about a herring supper – and left town in May 1873. In 1922, while their house still stood, a plaque was put on the outside wall – but it only mentioned Verlaine. Rimbaud was left off – for 'reasons of morality' – by some prudish authority. (Not long after this plaque was put up, another writer and artist moved in: Nina Hamnett. She lived in squalor there for some time, among lice and rat droppings and with newspaper bedding.)

Emile Zola (1840–1902) fled to London in 1898 following his famous 'J'Accuse' pronouncement on the corruption and anti-Semitism that had led to the false imprisonment of the army officer Alfred Dreyfus. Zola lived in Church Road, Upper Norwood, close to Crystal Palace – but the most telling story of his time in London comes from Ford Madox Ford, who found the writer in Hyde Park 'gazing gloomily at the ground and poking the sand with the end of his cane'. Zola went home as soon as he was able in 1899.

Fyodor Dostoevsky also had negative associations with Crystal Palace. When he visited in July 1862 – and although the Great Exhibition had shut its doors eleven years earlier – he railed against it as 'a terrible force that has united all the people here, who come from all over the world, into a single herd'. He didn't like the rest of London any better. In Haymarket, he was alarmed by how the locals stayed up until 5 a.m. on a Sunday night – and by the large numbers of prostitutes 'and their daughters'. He was also shocked when someone gave him a leaflet inviting him to join a Roman Catholic church and decried the 'shameless cynicism' of the crowd there. Whitechapel made him angrier still, 'with its half-naked, savage, and hungry population'. 'Everyone is drunk,' he complained. One night he recorded that he got lost and roamed the streets among crowds of 'dismal people'. The impression of what he saw haunted and tormented him afterwards. Then he left the capital for ever. He had only stayed eight days – but dedicated a whole chapter of his book *Winter Notes on Summer Impressions* to the visit. He entitled the chapter 'Baal' – after the false God of the Old Testament.

Not everyone was so negative. Visitors from the USA were especially complimentary about the capital when they started to flood in during the nineteenth century. Ralph Waldo Emerson (1803–82) declared after his stay in 1833 that:

> The best bribe which London offers to-day to the imagin -ation, is, that, in such a vast variety of people and conditions, one can believe there is room for persons of romantic charac- ter to exist, and that the poet, the mystic, and the hero may hope to confront their counterparts.

Herman Melville (1819–91) arrived in 1849, and he too had a whale of a time. He stayed in a boarding house at 25 Craven Street, near the Strand, but the real place of significance in his visit was Tower Hill. There he saw a beggar with a placard around his neck, featuring a crudely drawn picture of a whale – the one that had destroyed his ship and ruined his fortune. The idea for *Moby-Dick* was born.

It was Melville who also said: 'There are two places in the world where men can most effectively disappear – the city of London and the South Seas.' In 1897, a number of American newspapers took this quote rather too literally. Mark Twain (1835–1910) visited London on a lecture tour, hoping to raise money to pay his many debts back home – and a rumour began to spread in the US that he was dead. A man from the *New York Journal* eventually knocked on his door in Tedworth Square bearing two telegrams. The first read: 'If Mark Twain dying in poverty, send 500 words'. The second: 'If Mark Twain has died in pov- erty send 1000 words'. Twain famously responded: 'The report of my death was an exaggeration.'

No list of American visiting writers would be complete without Jack London – for obvious reasons. His time in the city inspired his 1903 publication *The People of the Abyss*, in which he declared: 'If this is the best civilization can do, then give us howling naked savagery.' He spent much of his time living in workhouses and slums in the East End of his namesake city, and the result was the biggest invective against the grinding poverty that so much of the London population had to endure since *The Condition of the Working Class in England* by Friedrich Engels (another immigrant and London-dweller) was published in 1845.

A few years later, Henry James, who had moved to England back in the 1860s, struggled to write his own guide to London. He bought a notebook with 140 pages, but filled only thirty-six with fragmentary notes in which he denounced various landmarks, describing, for instance, Tower Bridge as 'hideous' historical kitsch. He also noted: 'It is difficult to speak adequately or justly of London. It is not a pleasant place; it is not agreeable, or cheerful, or easy, or exempt from reproach. It is only magnificent. London is on the whole the most possible form of life.' Henry James does not recommend walking around much either:

> London is too monotonous and, in plain English, too ugly to supply that wayside entertainment which the observant pedestrian demands. The shabby quarters are too dusky, too depressing, English low life is too unrelieved by out-of-door picturesqueness, to be treated as a daily spectacle . . . On the other hand, the Squares and Crescents, the Roads and Gardens, are too rigidly, too blankly genteel . . . Buckingham Palace is lamentably ugly; St James's is less shabby only because it is less pretentious; Marlborough House is hidden away in a courtyard, and presents no face whatever to the world.

Guidebook writers are such fickle creatures.

Americans continued to visit, of course, throughout the twentieth century. Even the great poet of snowy rural life in New England, Robert Frost (1874–1963), once turned up at the famous Poetry Bookshop at 35 Boswell Street where the owner, Harold Munro, told him he could tell he was American because of his shoes. He asked Frost if he'd heard of Ezra Pound. Frost said no – and Munro warned him that he was, on no account, to say that to Pound's face.

In the twentieth century, London also benefited from a growing influx from elsewhere in the world, especially the Caribbean. One of the first was Jean Rhys, the (white creole) daughter of a family with rapidly diminishing fortunes, who set sail from Dominica in 1916, first boarding at the Perse School in Cambridge and then moving on to the Royal Academy of Dramatic Art, where she stayed for two terms, picked on by teachers and students alike for her heavily accented English. Although she is so often associated with 1920s Paris, Rhys spent more years in London, living in dingy boarding rooms or prettier mews houses in Kensington, depending upon her finances (and, largely, who she was married to at the time). There's a blue plaque at her Chelsea flat, Paultons House in Paultons Square (the same road Samuel Beckett lived in). She never forgot her disappointment on seeing Britain – and London – for the first time, with its grey skies and bleak pavements. 'London is like a cold dark dream,' she wrote – and with some justification, considering the poverty that she suffered there, as well as the snobbery and her mistreatment at the hands of London society.

After a long absence, Jean Rhys came back to London in 1964, to meet her editor Diana Athill for the first time and celebrate the near-completion of her late masterpiece *Wide Sargasso Sea*. The plan was that they would drink champagne in Rhys's hotel, but when Athill went there, she found a distraught manageress who told her that Rhys had suffered a heart attack. She met the author instead in hospital. Rhys lived to see the publication of her novel in 1966 – and widespread recognition, at last, of her genius.

The first novel by a black Caribbean author published in the UK was *Minty Alley* by the Trinidadian C. L. R. James (1901–89), published in 1936. James had moved to London in 1933, and spent the years until his death in and out of the city, writing about cricket, culture and left-wing politics – and sometimes combining the three with dazzling effect (as in his famous account of West Indian cricket, *Beyond a Boundary*). He died in Brixton in 1989, but his best memorial is the C. L. R. James Library on Dalston Lane in Hackney – a modernized version of a building whose opening he attended in 1985.

Soon after C. L. R. James came James Berry (1924–2017), a Jamaican poet who moved to London in the 1940s and started writing in a mixture of standard English and Jamaican patois. 'I knew I was right for London and London was right for me,' he later said. 'London had books and accessible libraries.'

Samuel Selvon (1923–94) broke further new ground in his 1956 novel *The Lonely Londoners* in his use of creolized English for narrative as well as dialogue – and in his focus on the migration of West Indians to the UK. It took him six months of struggling to write the book in standard English, before he had his great breakthrough and changed the language, using the perfectly London metaphor of riding on a bus to explain the process: 'I sat like a passenger . . . and let the language do the writing.'

'Daniel was telling him how over in France all kinds of fellars writing books what turn out to be bestsellers. Taxi-driver, porter, road-sweeper – it didn't matter. One day you sweating in the factory and the next day all the newspapers have your name and photo, saying you are a new literary giant.'

Samuel Selvon, *The Lonely Londoners*

In 1968, the poet and academic Edward Brathwaite (1930–2020) wrote an essay declaring that, within ten years of *The Lonely Londoners*, 'nearly every West Indian novelist worth the name had come to London'. He also noted that they'd produced more than 100 books since 1950 – and that the British public seemed all but unaware of the value of this contribution. In response, he set up the Caribbean Artists Movement in his flat in Mecklenburgh Square (home to Leonard and Virginia Woolf, decades earlier). Other big names quickly became involved, like the *New Left Review* founder Stewart Hall (1932–2014), and the movement went on to inspire a younger generation of writers such as Brixton-based Linton Kwesi Johnson (1952–) – the first black Jamaican poet to be published as a Penguin Classic.

Treading more of a lonely furrow was Trinidadian V. S. Naipaul, who said: 'I came to London [in 1954]. It had become the centre of my world and I had worked hard to come to it. And I was lost.' Lost or not, he published many of the books that would help earn him the 2001 Nobel Prize while living in the city.

The end of the twentieth century also saw a great flowering of books about the experience of immigrant families from the Indian subcontinent in London. One of the funniest takes comes in *The Buddha of Suburbia* by Hanif Kureishi (1954–), which is mostly set in Bromley, home to the 'miserable undead' where drowning men see double glazing flashing before them instead of their lives. More flattering is the description of the artistic and musical explosion the protagonist Karim Amir and his father witness in the Rat and Parrot on Beckenham High Street – inspired by Kureishi's real-life admiration for David Bowie and the Beckenham Arts Lab he established there at the end of the 1960s.

Zadie Smith (1975–) wrote with similar affectionate humour about the north-western suburb of Willesden in her all-conquering *White Teeth* and *NW*, describing, alongside families from all over the diaspora, confused Australians who find themselves 'inexplicably' in NW2 working in bars, far from their homeland with its silky beaches and emerald seas.

Closer to the centre, Monica Ali (1967–) earned a Booker short-listing for her depiction of Bangladeshi immigrants in *Brick Lane* in 2003 – although, of course, by this time a British Indian London resident, Salman Rushdie (1947–), had already won the Booker Prize with *Midnight's Children*, a novel he wrote while working at the advertising agency Ogilvy & Mather in Waterloo. At the same time, less notably, but also joyfully, he came up with the slogan 'irresistibubble' for Aero chocolate bars. It takes all sorts to make a world, after all.

KEY ADDRESSES

34 Howland Street, Fitzrovia, W1T (Tube station: Goodge Street)

25 Craven Street, WC2N (Tube station: Embankment)

37 Mecklenburgh Square, WC1N (Tube station: Russell Square)

Paultons House, 289 King's Road, SW3 (Tube station: Sloane Square)

19 King Charles Street, SW1A (Tube station: Westminster)

RECOMMENDED READING

Monica Ali, *Brick Lane*

Fyodor Dostoevsky, *Winter Notes on Summer Impressions*

C. L. R. James, *Minty Alley*; *Beyond a Boundary*

Hanif Kureishi, *The Buddha of Suburbia*

Jack London, *The People of the Abyss*

Samuel Selvon, *The Lonely Londoners*

Zadie Smith, *White Teeth*; *NW*

Voltaire, *Candide*

CHAPTER TWENTY-ONE

MONSTERS AND APOCALYPTICS

—⚭—

'And this also,' says the narrator of Joseph Conrad's *Heart of Darkness*, 'has been one of the dark places of the earth.' Marlow is looking down the river Thames as it stretches out to sea, thinking about 'very old times, when the Romans first came here, nineteen hundred years ago'. But he's also dwelling on the impermanence of civilization. 'We live in the flicker – may it last as long as the old earth keeps rolling!' he says. 'But darkness was here yesterday . . .'

Darkness, writers were beginning to realize, could also be here tomorrow. Just as Marlow was thinking of London before civilization, H. G. Wells was imagining its end – and depicting the smoke-blackened ruins of a capital destroyed by Martians in *The War of the Worlds*.

Published in 1897, Wells's masterpiece helped kick-start the science-fiction genre, while also building on a growing tradition of writers gleefully invading the capital.

This habit of laying into London began, strangely enough, in Switzerland, by the shores of Lake Geneva. There, in 1816, Mary Shelley, her husband Percy and friend John Polidori were visiting Lord Byron in his luxury house, Villa Diodati. The summer was cold and wet, thanks to the clouds cast by the eruption of Mount Tambora, half a world away. The friends were forced to remain inside, where they tried their hardest to make their surroundings more interesting by glugging laudanum and having a competition to see who could come up with the most frightening ghost story. When Byron's turn came, he opted for the urban legends and tales of blood-sucking he'd heard in the Balkans – stories which would inspire Polidori to write *The Vampyre*, published in 1819. *The Vampyre* describes Lord Ruthven, a man of origins unknown, seducing the cream of London society . . . and draining their blood. It would inspire dozens of pale and blood-thirsty imitators.

So too would Mary Shelley's *Frankenstein; or, The Modern Prometheus*, the novel she began after the same storytelling session. *Frankenstein* is mainly set around the shores of Lake Geneva, but one of her later books – *The Last Man*, from 1826 – tells the story of Lionel, a man making his way through London at the end of the twenty-first century . . . and the end of the known world. Lionel visits several London landmarks, among them Drury Lane Theatre, where he watches an emotional, omen-filled performance of *Macbeth* before plague strikes. Soon after, in Westminster Abbey, he sees a chorister drop dead – the poor boy 'consigned with a few muttered prayers' to hastily opened vaults below the Abbey floor ('the abode of thousands who had gone before – now wide yawning to receive even all who fulfilled the funeral rite'). It's gripping, grimy stuff, and Shelley depicts a haunted city of 'silent streets', a 'dread period' of 'tameless grief'. It was a template many writers would happily follow in the years to come.

> 'London did not contain above a thousand inhabitants; and this number was continually diminishing. Most of them were country people, come up for the sake of change; the Londoners had sought the country. The busy eastern part of the town was silent, or at most you saw only where, half from cupidity, half from curiosity, the warehouses had been more ransacked than pillaged: bales of rich India goods, shawls of price, jewels, and spices, unpacked, strewed the floor.'

Mary Shelley, *The Last Man*

In 1827, the year after *The Last Man* came out, Jane C. Loudon published a novel glorying in the title of *The Mummy!* (exclamation mark included). This 'tale of the twenty-second century' was part-inspired by the real-life public unwrapping of Egyptian mummies in 1821 in a theatre near Piccadilly, which the author saw as a girl – but it also had its origins in a line from *Frankenstein*: 'A mummy again endued with animation could not be so hideous as that wretch'.

Loudon clearly thought that mummies *could* be as hideous – and in *The Mummy!* she set about animating a bandage-wrapped corpse called Cheops, a 'fiend' who spends a good bit of his time back on earth giving advice on politics and individual rights (making this novel a pioneering work of early feminism, as well as fascinating early science fiction).

Monsters reared ugly heads again in the 1840s, as Londoners began to tuck into more and more 'Penny Dreadfuls'. These pamphlets weren't a new phenomenon. Sensationalist leaflets and spreads had been around and very popular in London since the sixteenth century, feeding the public's appetite for lurid tales of demons, witches and grisly murders. But they did enjoy something of a resurgence during the mid-nineteenth century, as printing costs dropped and publishers were able to provide more pages of story for the money. Whenever there was a good 'dreadful' running (the stories were published in weekly instalments), shops would find themselves beset on publication day with customers and unruly, excited queues. 'A world of dormant peerages, of murderous baronets, of ladies of title addicted to the study of toxicology,' was how one author, George A. Sala (1828–95), described their subject matter: 'Of gipsies and brigand chiefs, men with masks and women with daggers, of stolen children, withered hags, heartless gamesters.'

One especially popular serialization was James Malcolm Rymer (1814–84) and Thomas Peckett Prest's (1810–59) *Varney the Vampire*. By the time the instalments ended, the story was 876 pages long – and the plot, as you might expect from the name, involved setting yet another bloodsucker loose on the streets of London. (Rymer and Prest also invested Varney with many of the powers that would become essential parts of the vampire legend, including fanged teeth, hypnotic eyes and extraordinary superhuman strength.)

Another popular trope was introduced in 1885 when Richard Jeffries (1848–1887) submerged the city in *After London*. Here, civilization has collapsed (for unspecified reasons) and London lies under poisonous swamps – as is detailed in one vivid chapter, when the novel's protagonist paddles his canoe onto the site of the city and:

> . . . now at last began to realise his position; the finding of the heap of blackened money touched a chord of memory. These skeletons were the miserable relics of men who had ventured, in search of ancient treasures, into the deadly marshes over the site of the mightiest city of former days. The deserted and utterly extinct city of London was under his feet.

Alas!

Still greater shudders came the following year when another monster started roaming London, smacking innocents with his cane and pulling hideous facial expressions. It was the less savoury half of the split-personality hero of Robert Louis Stevenson's (1850–94) *The Strange Case of Dr Jekyll and Mr Hyde*.

Mr Hyde, we are told, lives in Soho: 'a dismal quarter . . . with its muddy ways, and slatternly passengers . . . like a district of some city in a nightmare'. The rest of London gets similar treatment, and even the city's green spaces offer little by way of refuge: 'Regent's Park was full of winter chirrupings and sweet with spring odours. I sat in the sun on a bench; the animal within me licking the chops of memory.'

Within two years of Mr Hyde's unsettling appearance, Jack the Ripper had begun his murder spree in the East End. This time, the monster was all too real – and, unlike in fiction, there was no happy ending. His crimes went unpunished, which in turn helped inspire endless conspiracy theories, several films and novels, and the *From Hell* comic by Alan Moore (1953–).

Jack the Ripper's penchant for young women and violent mutilation was also an inspiration for the most famous horror novel ever written: Bram Stoker's *Dracula*. Stoker wrote *Dracula* (which was published in 1897) while working as the manager of Henry Irving's Lyceum Theatre, just off the Strand (currently the home of Disney's London production of *The Lion King*). He'd moved to London at the end of the 1870s, living at 27 Cheyne Walk, near Albert Bridge in Chelsea – until a good deed put an end to his stay. Stoker rescued a drowning man from the Thames – diving in and pulling him out of the water, before arranging to have him taken back to his house. Unfortunately, by the time the man arrived at Cheyne Walk, he was dead. He was put on the dining-room table – at which point Stoker's wife came in. Understandably upset at seeing a corpse where she ate her dinner, she refused to stay in the house a minute longer, and the couple had to look for another place to live.

Such troubles aside, London invigorated the young Irish writer – just as it would his most famous creation. 'I long to go through the crowded streets of your mighty London,' Dracula tells Jonathan Harker in the novel, 'to be in the midst of the whirl and rush of humanity, to share its life, its change, its death, and all that makes it what it is.'

And share its life he does, in more ways than one. Harker at first arranges for Dracula to stay in a house in Purfleet on the eastern edge of London (next to the asylum where an inmate called Renfield enjoys eating flies), but Dracula eventually settles right in the heart of the city. Harker gets a terrible fright when, walking along Piccadilly, he sees 'a tall, thin man' who is staring at a pretty girl. 'His face was not a good face,' we are told: 'It was hard, and cruel, and sensual . . .'

As well as mixing with the gentry on Piccadilly, Dracula prowls the East End, around Whitechapel and (not coincidentally) the hunting grounds of Jack the Ripper. He causes a wolf to escape from London Zoo. His 'creature' Lucy Westenra lures children to Hampstead Heath at night to drink their blood. He has boxes of soil sent to Jamaica Lane, Bermondsey. Characters shop in Harrods. He takes a house overlooking Green Park and the 'Junior Constitutional Club' (probably based on the Junior Athenaeum, which was on the corner of Dow Street). He roams from one well-known site to another, and the novel draws tremendous power from this invasion of the familiar. Dracula's London is instantly recognizable – and seeing his shadowy form on those well-known streets makes him seem at once all the more real . . . and all the stranger.

H. G. Wells used the same mix of the familiar and the shocking in the aforementioned *The War of the Worlds*, published in the same year as *Dracula*. Wells actually has the alien invasion of Earth start in Surrey, on a common near Woking (where he was living at the time), but he soon moves the action up the Thames, past Hampton Court Palace, through Twickenham and Richmond (where the narrator sees its bridge covered in red Martian weed) on to Roehampton and Sheen. Here, the narrator spends several days hiding under a house, emerging to see 'the devastation of a cyclone' in safe old respectable Putney, before picking his way across the river, into Chelsea and then Kensington. Wells gleefully told a friend in a letter that he had especially selected this district 'for feats of peculiar atrocity' – and, among other things, he has locals killed midway through drinking bottles of champagne. Here too, in the shadow of the Natural History Museum, the narrator first hears the lament of the dying Martians: 'Ulla, ulla, ulla'. He sees their tripod devices towering empty over devastated streets and begins to understand that the aliens have lost, after all. Soon he moves on into Primrose Hill, taking a long lingering look over the shattered city. Beyond 'the green waves' of Regent's Park, he sees Westminster in 'jagged ruins' and the dome of St Paul's, dark against the rising sun, with 'a huge gaping cavity' on its western side.

> **'London, which had gone to bed on Sunday night oblivious and inert, was awakened, in the small hours of Monday morning, to a vivid sense of danger.'**
>
> H. G. Wells, *The War of the Worlds*

After this stunning vision it was dystopia and apocalypse every five minutes in London fiction. Hundreds of books have since been written about the destruction or transformation of

London and many of them have proved to be enduring classics.

Chief among them is George Orwell's *Nineteen Eighty-Four*, a dystopian vision of London as the capital of Airstrip One, watched over by Big Brother, ravaged by war and totalitarian brutality, but still recognizable. Trafalgar Square has become Victory Square (see p. 31). The huge Senate House (part of the University of London) on Malet Street is now the Ministry of Truth (this inspired by the years Orwell's wife Eileen Blair spent working there when it housed the Ministry of Information during the Second World War). Room 101 was based on a room at BBC Broadcasting House on Portland Place, where Orwell apparently used to sit through interminable meetings about political vetting.

Nineteen Eighty-Four was published in 1949. Two years after Orwell's terrifying vision, London enjoyed a rather more cosy catastrophe in the form of *The Day of the Triffids* by John Wyndham (1903–69). This time, anarchy is loosed on the city when the green light from a passing comet blinds most of its inhabitants – and, worse still, when huge carnivorous plants called triffids which are capable of movement start roaming around. The Senate House again performs a crucial role in the novel – but now a more benign one. A light is shone from its roof, signalling a safe meeting point for the few people who have kept their sight (including the protagonist Bill Masen and his love interest Josella, who he meets halfway up Regent Street), and allowing them to eventually escape the city and forge a new life.

In 1956, *The Death of Grass* inverted the idea of deadly flora. As the title of John Christopher's novel suggests, this time the problem is a lack of plant life. Christopher (1922–2012) has the 'Chung-Li virus' wipe out all wheats and grasses – and so endanger the world's food supply. The British government decides that the only way to preserve and feed a small part of the population is to kill the rest, so poor London is lined up for a hydrogen bomb. Roadblocks are set up on suburban streets, gunfights break out on the London section of the A1 – and the novel's protagonists flee north.

Abandoning the city became a popular trope in the nuclear age

– but post-apocalyptic London was not seen just as a place to be escaped. J. G. Ballard had many of his most famous characters positively embrace the chaos.

Writing from his semi-detached house on Old Charton Road in Shepperton, the SF sage followed Richard Jeffries in submerging the city in his 1962 novel *The Drowned World*, for instance. Only this time, some of the survivors of the apocalypse enjoy whooping it up in an abandoned Ritz Hotel – and cruising over the flooded landmarks of central London. The protagonist Dr Kerans is even outraged when attempts are made to drain the city and clear up the mess.

Elsewhere, Ballard had people embracing (in a very literal way) autogeddon near the Westway and in the concrete wasteland around Heathrow airport in *Crash*. And in *High-Rise*, the fact that a tower block on the eastern fringes of London reverted to barbarism was just seen as an excuse for more parties.

Yet more sybaritic are the monsters, politicians and debauched aristocrats gathering around Count Dracula and his wife Queen Victoria in *Anno Dracula*, an alternate history of the capital written in 1992 by Kim Newman (1959–). Buckingham Palace becomes the scene of blood-drenched orgies, Jack the Ripper takes to killing vampire prostitutes, both Dr Jekyll and Mr Hyde appear on the scene, along with Oscar Wilde and Beatrix Potter and dozens of other anti-heroes, authors and horrors from Victorian London.

This ability to enjoy the freedom of a world turned upside down was not shared by the lead character of *V for Vendetta*. Alan Moore's famous 'V' first appeared in a comic in 1982, behind a smile painted on a white mask. But the smile is deceptive. V is angry. Very angry. In his world, following a nuclear war, fascists have taken over the government and violent anarchy is the only way to resist. V plots the destruction of the Houses of Parliament and blows up landmarks like the Post Office Tower. He moves through a dangerous London drawn in thick black shades, and lives in the shadows – in the Shadow Gallery, in fact, to give the precise name for his lair beneath Victoria Railway Station.

Underground London also featured in a mid-1990s classic from Neil Gaiman (1960–). *Neverwhere* is a book about people who have fallen 'through the cracks in the world' and ended up in an alternate city below the original. It was inspired by questions Gaiman used to ask himself while travelling on the Tube: Is there actually an Earl at Earl's Court Station? Is there an Angel at Islington? Who are the Seven Sisters? And how deep down does Down Street go? ('Down Street' is a disused station in Mayfair, which was used as Winston Churchill's wartime bunker.)

More recently, Louise Welsh (1965–) has laid waste to London with a new form of plague in 2014's *A Lovely Way to Burn*. It has also been drenched again in 2004's *The Flood* by Maggie Gee (1948–) and Will Self's (1961–) 2006 novel, *The Book of Dave*. In this latter, all that remains of the lost city is a religion based on the rantings of a cab driver called Dave and his knowledge of the lost capital. The rest is underwater.

And so literature takes London back to its very beginnings as a watery waste and one of the dark places of the earth. All those people, all that memory, all those words and books, gone to nothing ...

ACKNOWLEDGEMENTS AND ADDITIONAL READING

—w—

T hank you to Hugh Barker, Gabriella Nemeth and everyone at Michael O'Mara Books and to Susan Smith and all our friends at MBA. We are also grateful to Steve Finbow, who gave us some fine information on the Beats and cool things in London in the second half of the twentieth century. It would also be impossible to write a book like this without the benefit of the research and hard work of generations of writers before us. We have relied not only on original novels, plays, poems and diaries, but on the many excellent guidebooks to London. The following is a small selection of those that were most useful and enjoyable. We salute and thank them.

ADDITIONAL READING

Peter Ackroyd, *London: A Biography*

Harold Bloom, *Bloom's London*

Ian Cunningham, *A Writer's Guide to Literary London*

Ed Glinert, *A Literary Guide to London; The London Compendium;* and *West End Chronicles*

Rudiger Gorner, *London in Fragments*

Daniel Hahn and Nicholas Robins, *The Oxford Guide to Literary Britain*

Stephen Halliday, *From 221B Baker Street to the Old Curiosity Shop*

Barry Miles, *London Calling: A Countercultural History of London Since 1945*

Anna Quindlen, *Imagined London*

D. J. Taylor, *The Prose Factory*

Virginia Woolf, *The London Scene*

For specific periods, schools and specific writers, not to be missed are:

Peter Ackroyd, *Blake*

Alexander Larman, *Blazing Star (The Life and Times of John Wilmot, Earl of Rochester)*

Hermione Lee, *Virginia Woolf*

Andrew Lycett, *Rudyard Kipling*

Virginia Nicholson, *Among the Bohemians: Experiments in Living 1900–1939*

Norman Sherry, *The Life of Graham Greene*

D. J. Taylor, *George Orwell*

Claire Tomalin, *Charles Dickens: A Life*; *The Life and Death of Mary Wollstonecraft*

Fine internet resources include:

The Londonist: www.londonist.com

David Perdue's www.charlesdickenspage.com

Exploring Twentieth Century London:
   www.20thcenturylondon.org.uk

The Shady Old Lady's Guide to London: www.shadyoldlady.com

The Deighton Dossier: www.deightondossier.blogspot.co.uk

INDEX

—m—

A

Ackroyd, Peter 42, 45, 55
Aldington, Richard 129
Alfred the Great 9
Ali, Monica 208
Allsop, Kenneth 184
Amis, Kingsley 165, 167, 168
Amis, Martin 81, 168
Angry Young Men 158, 165–170
Archer, David 169
Astell, Mary 172
Athill, Diana 162, 206

B

Ball, John 27, 28
Ballard, J.G. 217
Banks, Lynne Reid 181
Barnes, Djuna 126
Barnes, Julian 81
Barrett Browning, Elizabeth 87
Barrie, J.M. 114–116
Bauer, Edgar 30
Beaton, Cecil 140
Beats 184–187
Beckett, Samuel 130, 158, 206
Behn, Aphra 172
Belcher, Muriel 169
Bell, Clive 125, 132, 133, 136
Bell, Vanessa 125, 132, 133, 136
Belloc, Hilaire 36–37
Benn, Tony 54
Bennett, Alan 55
Bernard, Jeffrey 147
Berry, James 207
Besant, Annie 177
Betjeman, John 140
Better Books 158–159
Blake, William 35, 42–44, 151

Bloomsbury Group 132–138
Blyton, Enid 116
Bond, Michael 120–122
Boswell, James 51, 173
Bowen, Elizabeth 126, 192
Bowie, David 189, 208
Boyars, Marion 158
Braine, John 33, 165, 166, 167
Brathwaite, Edward 207
Bright Young Things 140–142
Brittain, Vera 54
Brontë, Charlotte 87–89
Browning, Robert 87
Buchan, John 191, 192, 193
Bulwer-Lytton, Edward 83
Bunyan, John 35
Burgess, Anthony 14, 145, 146, 162, 184
Burroughs, William 185, 186
Byron, Lord 59–60, 64, 65, 66, 70, 71, 152, 160, 162, 176, 177, 210–211

C

Calder, John 158, 185
Callil, Carmen 162–163,
Carter, Angela 182
Caxton, William 10, 155
Chapman, John 89, 90
Chatterton, Thomas 65, 66
Chaucer, Geoffrey 8, 10–12, 39, 108, 139
Chesterton, G.K. 37, 59, 96, 99, 100, 101, 191
Christie, Agatha 100, 102–104
Christopher, John 216
Cleland, John 107
Cobbett, William 31, 108
Coleridge, Samuel Taylor 65, 66, 67, 69, 72–73
Collins, Wilkie 82–84, 96
Conrad, Joseph 59, 112, 191, 210

INDEX